LISA YVETTE PEARSON, M.DIV.

RETURN TO HOLINESS

BLACK CHURCH BEGINNINGS AND WHY WE NEED A REMIX TODAY

Copyright © 2025 Lisa Yvette Pearson

Printed in the United States of America

ISBN: 978-0-9827837-1-9

All rights reserved solely by the author. The author guarantees all contents are original and do not infringe upon the legal rights of any other person or work. No part of this book may be reproduced, stored in a retrieval system, or transmitted in any form or by any means without expressed written permission of the author.

Scripture quotations marked (AMP) are taken from the Amplified Bible, Copyright © 2015 by The Lockman Foundation. Used by permission.

Scripture quotations are from the ESV® Bible (The Holy Bible, English Standard Version®), © 2001 by Crossway, a publishing ministry of Good News Publishers. Used by permission. All rights reserved. The ESV text may not be quoted in any publication made available to the public by a Creative Commons license. The ESV may not be translated in whole or in part into any other language."

Scripture quotations marked (NIV) are taken from the Holy Bible, New International Version®, NIV®. Copyright © 1973, 1978, 1984, 2011 by Biblica, Inc.™ Used by permission of Zondervan. All rights reserved worldwide. www.zondervan.com The "NIV" and "New International Version" are trademarks registered in the United States Patent and Trademark Office by Biblica, Inc.™

Scripture taken from the New King James Version®. Copyright © 1982 by Thomas Nelson. Used by permission. All rights reserved.

Scripture quotations marked (NLT) are taken from the Holy Bible, New Living Translation, copyright ©1996, 2004, 2015 by Tyndale House Foundation. Used by permission of Tyndale House Publishers, Carol Stream, Illinois 60188. All rights reserved.

Published by Lisa Yvette Pearson
Instagram: @startingover_withlisa

Cover design and page formatting: Lisa Pearson
Cover photo courtesy of Canva AI and Lisa Pearson

Dedication

Pastor Charles Evans (1944-2024)

Acknowledgments

I'd like to thank God for seeing in me the things I couldn't. Thank You for opening my eyes to see holiness as You do. Thank You for stripping me of those things that are not like You, for equipping me, and for consoling and encouraging me through the difficult days. Thank You for the joyous days and peace that comes in You. Thank You for Your sacrifice and for loving me with an everlasting love. Your love is incomparable.

Thank you to my parents and my family for all their love and support.

Thank you to every pastor, elder, church sister and brother who has prayed for, taught, and poured into me on this journey.

Thank you to every friend who has encouraged, checked in, or lifted my name up for prayer.

Thank you to every professor and instructor for sharing your expertise and insight of Christ and all of scripture. Thank you to all who challenged, encouraged, and had grace for me in seminary.

Thank you to any and everyone who has whispered my name to God or bombarded heaven on my behalf, praying for His promises for my life. May the blessings you prayed for me be multiplied unto you.

Table of Contents

I. Introduction
    Holiness is Still Right   1

II. The History of the Perversion of Holiness
    The Biblical History of The Perversion   9
    The Black History of The Perversion   17

III. The Tradition of Churchiness: An Enemy of Holiness
    Churchiness is a Preference   35
    The Dangers of Churchiness   38
    Holiness, Control, and Manipulation   49
    Jesus & The Churchy Holy Men   62

IV. Why Holiness Matters
    Holiness & the Holy Spirit   71

V. The Re-Introduction to Holiness
    In All Things Get Understanding of God   79
    Who You Are to God   107
    Who You Are in Christ   111
    The Pure Heart   119
    Final Words   124

I. Introduction

ଔ

Holiness is Still Right

THE TEA IN THE BLACK CHURCH TODAY is that holiness has left the group chat. Complaints vary depending on who you ask: *It's become theatrical. The megachurches have big screens. The lights and the smoke machines are too much. They don't mention Jesus. It's no longer the Gospel, it's motivational speeches. There are no hymns. We need to get back to holiness. Holiness is still right.*[1]

There may be some truth to this. Theatrics in various forms have, indeed, become a part of some Sunday sermons. But if we're being truthful, all that hootin' and hollerin' that some preachers do is in part because some of us only respond to the gravelly type of preaching that's followed by a *"ha!"* and a deep inhale after every sentence. Preacher gets whipped up into a frenzy and, in turn, whips the church up into a frenzy

---

1   "Holiness is still right" is a church term that is used in the Black Church when someone "holy" critiques the behavior of a wayward saint or commends a church leader who has made a declaration that is deemed biblically sound. We also like to say it when a sin is called out. But some of it is a judgment made by some who aren't so holy themselves.

that seems like holiness. That's not judgment, it's an observation that for some of us, some theatrics are just fine. But it has escalated. And that's where we are now.

Demonstrations and performances are over the top. The musicians warm up the crowd and everyone stands to welcome the man of God who comes from backstage like your favorite superstar. Cultural relevance has been pushed to the front while Jesus is pushed to the back. For the record, "They Not Like Us" has no relevance to the Gospel of Jesus Christ.

In the past, these things may have only been seen by the local body, but with live streaming these exhibitions have gone worldwide - full scale productions with fire and big screen graphics. *But has holiness gone worldwide?*

The real question is, can we even identify it? It cannot be determined by how big or small the congregation. Or by whether or not the women wear skirts to their ankles and the men wear suits. Is holiness marked by whether or not a preacher calls down the brimstone and the fires of hell on everyone, every week? Can you tell if holiness is present in one's church because they don't use technology? By whether or not a church uses a big screen to display the worship song or if they use a hymnal? Remember that many called Facebook "the devil" (unholy) until the church doors closed in 2020. Just because something is new or we don't understand does not make it unholy. As for needing to get back to holiness, this will always be true for each and every one of us. Holiness is still right. To get there, we can't church how we've always been churching.

But what is holiness?

Google and Concordance[2] Definition

According to Google, holiness means "the state of being holy." Holy is defined as "dedicated or consecrated to God or a religious purpose" or "sacred." The Bible concordance says that the Hebrew word for holy is *qadosh* (pronounced kaw-dosh) which means "sacred, Holy One, saint, set apart as it relates to God (by eminence), an angel, a saint, a sanctuary..." The other Hebrew word is *qodesh* (pronounced ko-desh) which means "apartness, sacredness, separateness" of God, of places, of things). This "holy" is used when we read about the Holy Spirit in the Old Testament. Lastly, the Greek word for holy is *agios* (pronounced ah-ghee-oss) which means sacred (physically, pure, morally blameless or religious, ceremonially, consecrated). This "holy" is used when we read about the Holy Spirit in the New Testament.

World Definition

Outside of church circles, holiness can be associated with the church, organized religion and its practices, a religious title or office, or a deity. It could be derogatory, like when someone who is morally responsible or self-righteous is accused of being "holier than thou."

Church Definition

So among Christians, it would not be unusual to find that we, too, have different definitions or different ideas of

---

2 Strong's Concordance and/or Blue Letter Bible apps (as well as others) are available on your Apple or Android platforms.

what constitutes holiness. All may agree that it has to do with God, godliness, and being "holy." However, many would say that holiness has to do with the clothes women wear, the words one speaks, how much scripture one knows, how serious or pious one is, or the public activities in which one participates. But some Christians publicly behave one way among Christians and another way among non-Christians, another way when among a trusted friend or family group, and an entirely different way when alone. There are, obviously, rules of etiquette for certain places and some behaviors that are private that are not necessarily unholy. Nevertheless, clothing, speech, and public activity are typically used as an outer indication of holiness while those things can simply be the socially acceptable markers one uses to appear holy.

That, my sisters and brothers, is what needs inspection. It's possible that our measurements of holiness are off considering our history which will be discussed. Thus, we aren't gauging holiness correctly for ourselves or others. If that's the case, we are missing the mark; inadvertantly choosing the appearance of holiness over actual holiness.

The Big Question

Why choose to appear holy over actually being holy?

It's easier. The cross is heavy and the weight is sometimes overwhelming when we desire holiness. The consecration that comes with being holy kills all idols; especially the ones we actively worship, like comfort, stability, vanity, and sin.

Ignorance. If one doesn't read the Bible, how would one even begin to identify what is holy? How might they discern the pastor's words or actions as holy? So in ignorance, because there is nothing on which to gauge the holiness God exhibits, many *imitate* the people who say the churchiest things and wear the churchiest clothing and call it holy.

For acceptance. Church is very much like other social settings that have its own culture and rules of engagement. One can be pushed out if they don't conform to so-called holiness - even if just externally.

Deception. How a person is perceived determines access. The devil appears as an angel of light for the purpose of gaining access to your soul. One who "appears" holy can more easily deceive and corrupt that which God desires to actually be holy.

It's been taught and modeled. Historically, holiness has been corrupted for the Black Church since its start and it has traveled through generations; from slavery to Reconstruction to the Jim Crow era to the Civil Rights Movement to now. Seeds of misinterpretation, manipulation, and control were planted and have grown like weeds. Being a hypocrite and teaching as a hypocrite has also been taught and modeled. But hypocrisy indicates deceit. Holiness cannot preside there.

Unbeknownst to us, there are repercussions for practicing the appearance of holiness over the actual. The first repercussion results in a church split or exodus from the church. Integrity does matter. But the far more prevalent repercussion is where appearing holy rather than actual holiness can become the culture and standard practice of the church, from leadership down to the Body.

Those examples help us understand how this behavior can be normalized in the church and why we repeat churchy sayings like *"Holiness is still right"* without being clear on the meaning of holiness.

Holiness can only be deemed right if holiness is, first, rightly able to be identified. Too many presume to easily identify holiness or a lack thereof, by churchy standards, not by the sweet savor of He who is holy. God is calling His church, those who desire to be renewed by His Spirit, back to holiness because there are too many lives saved, but not transformed.

It wasn't until 2016, when the late Pastor Charles Evans pronounced, "We don't offer you church. We offer you Jesus" that I realized there was a difference and, recently, that many of us are ignorant of that, and the church needs a remix.

A remix is generally another version of a song with a new beat. We've got some parts of the holiness song right, but holiness needs a reintroduction with a new beat.

Obviously there are people who have a strong conviction of the Holy Spirit and live a life of holiness. But there are far too many who don't; who do church, not Christ.

Just know, we didn't get to this place on a whim. Let's explore where we've been as a church, how holiness was perverted from our first introduction, and why the remix of what we believe to be holiness is necessary.

II. The History of the Perversion of Holiness

III. The Reverse, the
Perversion of Holiness

☙

The Biblical History of The Perversion

Perversion: the alteration of something from its original course, meaning, or state to a distortion or corruption of what was first intended.[1]

How did holiness get perverted in the Black Church? Oppression is the root cause of how holiness was perverted in the Black Church. Oppression is rooted in sin in the form of greed, pride and lust of the flesh. It accounts for the kidnapping and subjugation of the enslaved Africans and the development of the Jim Crow South - all of which have taken a toll on the African-American psyche and spiritual lens.

However, perversion of holiness is not only a Black Church problem. Perversion of holiness is biblical and is, thus, universal to the church. Wherever sin (humanity!) is present, there is room for misunderstanding and error. There are, however, specific eras throughout the centuries that de-

---

[1] Google, Oxford Languages Dictionary.

veloped a perversion specific to the enslaved Africans in the United States of America and the Caribbean. But first, let's look biblically.

Old Testament
- Aaron's sons *"died [in the presence of God] when they offered [in their ceremonial censers] strange [unholy, unacceptable, unauthorized] fire before the Lord."* (Num. 26:61, AMP)
- In the land of milk and honey, Israelites worshiped the Canaanite gods and kept Asherah poles and images of Ashtoreth intact (1 Ki. 15:13, 2 Ki. 21:7, 2 Ki. 23:4, 13, 2 Chr. 15:16) despite God's laws and statutes to be holy.
- King Solomon worshiped the gods of his many wives which caused all but the kingdom of Judah to be ripped from his hands. (1 Ki. 11:33)

Aaron's sons perverted holiness by adding what was not specified by God. The Israelites openly defied God's command which is opposition to holiness. King Solomon submitted to his flesh, opposing God's call to holiness.

New Testament
In the New Testament, Jesus rebuked synagogue leaders who oppressed others under the facade of holiness. (Mt. 23, Lk. 13:15, Jn. 5:37-47) Later, John rebuked five out of the seven early churches in Revelation 2-3 for sins against holiness that the church continues to struggle with. Let's look.

1. **The Church of Ephesus** left their first love: Jesus. Lest we forget, God first loved us. (1 Jn. 4:19) Love begins with Him. He is the Gospel and brings the Gospel. Without the Gospel, there is no love for Jesus or those He's commissioned us to love as He has loved us. They left Jesus. They left love. And holiness.

2. **The Church at Pergamos** was located where Satan dwelled, yet they kept their faith. (Rev. 2:13) However, they compromised by holding *"to the teaching of Balaam who taught Balak to entice the Israelites to sin so that they ate food sacrificed to idols and committed sexual immorality. Likewise, you also have those who hold to the teaching of the Nicolaitans."* (Rev. 2:14-15 NIV) Balaam was a diviner (Num. 22:7) and a prophet. (Num. 22:8) God spoke to him. (Num. 22:12) God consistently reminded him to only do or say what He told him to. (Num. 22:20, 35) But he nearly met death in agreeing to go with Balak because he lost his discernment of God (Num. 22:23-34) in pursuit of receiving a reward that ultimately did not come. (Num. 24:11)

In 2 Peter 2:15 (NIV) it says, Balaam *"loved the wages of wickedness."* Jude 1:11 (NIV) says the ungodly *"have rushed for profit into Balaam's error."* The leaders taught for profit or "filthy lucre" (2 Tim. 3:8) which caused the church to compromise (using divination and/or prophetic gift) which lead the Body to sin. The passage also says this compromised church held to the teaching of the Nicolaitans (*nikolaites*): destruction of the people. Destruction: no holiness.

3. **The Church at Thyatira** was corrupt, though they had works of *"love, service, faith, and patience;"* (Rev. 2:19). However, the church was corrupted because they allowed *"that woman Jezebel, who calls herself a prophetess, to teach and seduce My servants to commit sexual immorality and eat things sacrificed to idols."* (Rev. 2:20). In other words, they allowed someone (who appointed herself) to manipulate the people and lead them to sin - away from holiness. [Note: The sins at both Thyatira and Pergamos included sexual immorality and eating food sacrifice to idols. Corruption came at the hands of both a man and a woman. Selah.]

4. **The Church of Sardis** was dead. (Rev. 3:1) The scripture says, *"Remember, therefore, how you have received and heard; hold fast and repent"* which implies they'd forgotten how they'd formerly received revelation from the Lord and what they'd heard from Him, instead relying on the flesh. The Spirit was quenched and the Living Water was not the stream from which they were drinking. No Holy Spirit, no holiness.

5. **The Church of the Laodiceans** received the rebuke of being a lukewarm church who no longer strived after God's desire because their material needs were covered. (Rev. 3:17) He invited the Laodiceans to buy of Him so that may be made truly rich and receive eyes to see. (Rev. 3:18) When we no longer strive after God's desires and focus on our own, how might holiness persist?

So you see, since biblical times, we have consistently edged God - and thus, holiness - out of our churches. But God consistently invites us to repent and come back to Him.

You will read this numerous times, so try not to get annoyed: No church is immune to these behaviors, but we are focused on the Black Church which is, and always has been, more than just a worship place. It was also, and still is, part of the social fabric in many communities. Community food pantries, soup kitchens, daycares, and outreach programs have come out of the Black Church. But like our predecessors in the churches of Revelation 2-3, we lose sight and hearing of God, misunderstand the purpose of the church and ministry, and focus, not on God and worship and transformation, but on works like Martha, and on our emotional and material needs.

Given the hardship of many of our ancestors, one would absolutely need to hear that God is going to *"supply all our needs according to His riches in glory."* One would need to hear, *"In my Father's house there are many mansions."* One would need to hear that *"vengeance is the Lord's"* and desire to see all those things immediately! Don't we pray a "right now" prayer when we meet difficulty? *I need You now, God!* For some, the promise of material improvement, the emotionalism of the service, and a specific criteria of what God could do/had done for them materially would become the measure of faith. Church would also be the place where one could outwardly express the pain that likely had to be contained. The music and the right words from the preacher would draw it out. But when emotion is gone or God's answer is not what was expected, do we still have faith? The perversion we witness in scripture is because of humanity's propensity to, first, believe the enemy's voice over God's voice, and second, to lean to our own understanding. It started in the Garden and continues in all the earth. Why? Because we lose focus.

Many, like some of the seven churches, have lost focus of what we sow mentally and spiritually into becoming like Christ: the holiness. We were (and are still) having the emotions and getting "all the things" which can be attained whether one believes in God or not. But are we changed?

With God, we can persevere. But are we changed?

The true change, better yet, the transformation that Christ offers lies in holiness. The supernatural power of holiness - being led by the Holy Spirit and living according to God's written statutes and commandments as well as the whispers and nudges of the Spirit extends healing beyond the body to renewal of the mind. And when we fall short, we re-pent. With holiness, we no longer conform to the ways of the world. The transformation via surrender to God and His desire for holiness breaks strongholds and frees families from generational turmoil, sin, and warfare.

We must surrender, lest we end up where we started: enslaved. We cannot afford to perpetuate the cycle of the corrupted church. We cannot afford to merely appear holy anymore.

ଔ

The Black History of The Perversion

HISTORICALLY, ENSLAVED AFRICANS AS A WHOLE were controlled under the pretense of a "Christian" moral code. During the Trans-Atlantic Slave Trade of 1619-1867, slave owners in the Americas and Caribbean perverted scripture to justify subjugating the stolen and enslaved Africans.

According to Time Magazine, slave owners used the "Curse of Ham" from Gen. 9:18-27 and Eph. 6:5-7 as justification for slavery. In the British West Indies, parts of the Bible about freedom and rebellion (including the book of Exodus) were removed so that the British missionaries could convert the enslaved, but avoid rebellion.[2] It's been assumed that all slave owners sought to convert enslaved Africans to Christianity, however this was not immediately the case. Believe it or not, their Christian beliefs temporarily deterred them.

What the enslaved were taught, however, was corrupt-

---

2.   https://www.npr.org/2018/12/09/674995075/slave-bible-from-the-1800s-omitted-key-passages-that-could-incite-rebellion

ed. Initially, all the enslaved Africans had were teachings that were redacted (edited or redefined, and thus misinterpreted) for the slave owner's advantage and peace of mind. Where there is pretense and redaction, there is corruption.

A Corrupted Introduction

In Deuteronomy 4:1, God tells Israel that He is about to teach them laws and decrees for their own success. But He warns them in the next verse, *"Do not add to what I command you and do not subtract from it, but keep the commands of the Lord your God that I give you."* (Deut. 4:2)

In the same way, God has given us scripture to follow for us to be successful - meaning to become more like Him. To remove, add to, or selectively misinterpret what God has said would be to corrupt it. This is precisely what happened. This introduction to Christianity, and thus, the introduction to holiness was corrupted. Thus, the corruption of the Black Church began way before the its inception. Let's take a look.

1400's

In the early part of the slave trade that began in Portugal, Africans who lived on the coast in the 15th century were introduced to Christianity by missionaries from Portugal.

1600's

In 1619, the first ship containing kidnapped and enslaved people of Angolan descent, docked in America at Point Comfort in the colony of Virginia. When forced into slavery, those who'd previously converted to Christianity brought their beliefs with them.[3] Otherwise, many slaves brought to the Americas and West Indies did not immediately, if at all, convert to Christianity.

1700's

There was, however, a segment of the enslaved who converted by this time because they thought they'd be freed. It might have been done sooner, but many slave owners were hesitant in converting and baptizing the slaves. In the book, *Vital American Problems: An Attempt to Solve the Trust, Labor, and Negro Problems*, Harry Earl Montgomery said:

> *The two centuries of American slave trade had destroyed the tribal life of the African coast Negroes and had brought about the mingling of clans and of religious beliefs which resulted in a chaos of religious ideas. [...]These pagan beliefs were allowed to grow practically unchecked and unmodified, because of the widespread idea that it was contrary to law to hold Christians as slaves, and the masters were more attached to their property than they were interested in the spread of the gospel in which they professed to believe.[4]*

---

3   https://www.thirteen.org/wnet/slavery/experience/religion/history.html

4   Montgomery, Harry Earl. Vital American Problems: An Attempt to Solve the Trust, Labor, and Negro Problems. United Kingdom, Putnam, 1908, 306

What a conundrum to be in: enact the command of Mt. 28:19-20 that says, *"Therefore go and make disciples of all nations, baptizing them in the name of the Father and of the Son and of the Holy Spirit, and teaching them to obey everything I have commanded you..."* or keep men, women, and children as property and maintain one's financial footing.

However, in 1706, the northern colony of New York passed a law that alleviated that tension. It said, in essence, that the enslaved Black, Mulatto, or Indigenous person could be baptized, but would not be considered free. And thus the dilemma was solved, but a new one soon came. Montgomery says:

> *Other colonies followed the example of New York by declaring that the Christian baptism of the Negro had no effect on the master's right and title to own and hold him as slave and chattel. The result of these acts was that a large number of slaves applied for admission into the Christian Church. So great became the number of Negro Christians that the question arose as to whether it would be wiser to allow the master and slave to worship in the same church, or to permit the slaves to have churches of their own. Both plans were adopted. Soon, however, the masters began to fear the effect of the regular meeting of slaves, and in 1715 North Carolina passed an act which declared:*

> *"That if any master or owner of Negroes or slaves, or any other person or persons whatsoever in the government, shall permit or suffer any Negro or Negroes to build on their, or either of their, lands, or any part thereof, any house under pretense of a meeting-house upon account of worship, or upon any pretense whatsoever, and shall not suppress or hinder them, he, she, or they so offending, shall for every default, forfeit and pay fifty pounds, one-half toward defraying the contingent charges of the government, and the other to him or them that shall sue for the same."* [5]

Because of this, white citizens actively policed or shut down any Black Churches that were erected. In addition, the Oakland Literacy Coalition says that there were anti-literacy laws put in place in Southern slave states from 1740-1834 following a slave rebellion in South Carolina in 1739. The laws, created out of fear of another uprising, made it illegal to teach enslaved or free Africans to read or write.[6] This would limit communication between slaves on different plantations. It would also limit who could read scripture to confirm or deny what was taught - further creating a perversion of holiness.

---

5   Montgomery, 306.
6   https://oaklandliteracycoalition.org/literacy-by-any-means-necessary-the-history-of-anti-literacy-laws-in-the-u-s/#

1800's

Even with the forced "migration" of enslaved Africans into Christianity,

> "As late as 1800 most slaves in the U.S. had not been converted to Christianity. In the years that followed, however, widespread Protestant Evangelicalism, emphasizing individual freedom and direct communication with God, brought about the first large-scale conversion of enslaved men and women." [7]

By 1831, three years prior to the end of anti-literacy laws, laws were passed in Virginia, North Carolina, Maryland, Georgia, and Mississippi that prohibited Negroes from preaching. In Mississippi, the consequence was thirty-nine lashes if they met without permission. If they did get permission, it required there were six white slave owners in attendance.[8] Laws in Alabama were just as restrictive. The beginnings of Black Church were rife with scriptural perversion and policing. Still, Montgomery says that as of 1859, despite these difficulties, 468,000[9] black people registered as church members.

---

[7] https://www.thirteen.org/wnet/slavery/experience/religion/history2.html

[8] Montgomery, 307.

[9] Montgomery, 309.

Reconstruction (1861-1900)

After the Civil War (1861-1865), any enslaved people who attended a white church were ousted. The good thing was that they had options, particularly in the Methodist Church because of the many splits that came about; the African Methodist Episcopal Church being the most prominent in the South. According to Clarence E. Walker, the church's aim was to get "souls and church property."[10] But there was also a need for belonging and a sense of freedom that came with joining the church of one's own choosing. Walker says,

> "in a society in which religion played a prominent role, church membership and attendance were signs of respectability. To be without a church affiliation was to occupy a second-class status in many southern communities. Therefore, when a slave left his master's church, he took an important step in defining himself as a free man and as a responsible member of the community in which he resided."[11]

By this time, the United States was trying to figure out what this new landscape was going to look like. The Confederate states who'd seceded, the Union, and freed black people had a new course to navigate. How would it work together? With tons of conflict. The Ku Klux Klan emerged in opposi

---

10   Walker, Clarence E. "The A.M.E. Church and Reconstruction." Negro History Bulletin, vol. 48, no. 1, 1985, pp. 10–12. JSTOR, http://www.jstor.org/stable/44176613. Accessed 24 July 2024.

11   Walker, 10.

tion to black people having voting rights and taking public office.

They instituted poll taxes and literacy tests as obstacles to rights that had been signed into law. Still, churches flourished, and black people clambered to be educated. By 1903, membership in Black Churches of various denominations came in at 3,522,843[12] members and 1,259[13] theological graduates were recorded as having matriculated from designated black schools founded between 1867 and 1892, most of which we currently know as HBCUs.[14] The end of slavery, new constitutional laws and rights, the rise in (theological) education, and even participation in politics should have been the end of the confusion, but no. While black people were building their own schools, establishments, and holding public office, the lynching era and Jim Crow brought about further conflict in the community and the Black Church.

Jim Crow

Suffering and persecution persisted in order to keep black people submitted to white supremacy. The Black Church had a role to play. Theologian James Cone says that keeping hope and faith in the midst of the "lynching era (1880-1940)"[15] were "the challenges that shaped black religious life in America."[16]

12   Montgomery, 310.
13   Montgomery, 311.
14   Montgomery, 310-311.
15   Cone, James H.. The Cross and the Lynching Tree. United States, Orbis Books, 2011, 3.
16   Cone, 3.

This was a time when there were no true legal repercussions for white citizens when it came to their treatment of the African-American. They could enter any black space without permission or punishment. To protest their actions meant the victim(s) could be arrested or lynched or have their homes burned to the ground as both a punishment to them and a warning to anyone else who considered doing the same.

While strengthening the faith of some, this kind of confusion is catastrophic to the formation or maturation of one's faith and damaging to the perception of what leadership looks like. At this stage, the corruption of biblical text spread in a different way; this time not for nefarious purposes, but for survival. Negro spirituals evolved from scripture both as the intention of providing hope as well providing an outlet for sorrow through "sorrow songs" despite questionable interpretation.[17]

AN INNER BATTLE

What kind of turmoil must the black believer have faced? *We have accepted this God by grace. But how can we believe in a just God when there seems to be no justice? How do I reconcile the hatred by and for my white brothers and sisters in Christ? Forgiveness? How?*

Many still believed and held on to the hope of Jesus and eternal life. But with all the surveillance, there may have also (sub)consciously been the question of *what must our*

---

17   Lynne, Sandra. "Black Church Culture and Community Action." Social Forces (2005): n. pag. Print. 970.

worship or behavior look like in order to be acceptable to the white gaze; to not draw suspicion?

The unconscious question that comes up when socialized (trained to behave or respond in a certain way in a specific social culture) in this way is: *when in a position of power, how do we run a church with these models of leadership?*

The Question is...

Did they ask the question? Or did they do what most people do and, instead, mimic what had been modeled? As we've already explored, black citizens, even within the walls of the Black Church, were heavily policed. Remember that six respected white slave holders had to be present for a church service to be allowed. Certainly, the message had to be carefully constructed. I would speculate, too, that "Sunday's best" was required. Control of external perception, executed for what we might consider safety reasons, must have been the name of the game. We still do it. We've learned over the years, however, that the most professional-looking of black professionals will still experience micro and full-fledged aggressions from white counterparts at work, be pulled over, or arrested despite "modest" or professional apparel. Meanwhile, we hold to respectability politics for the sake of acceptance and use it as a marker to classify one another as holy or not-so-much.

Let's consider, too, the complexity of when someone lives through this corrupted version of church and Christianity and how they view God and leadership roles.

How easy would it be for church leaders who have only

seen leadership through the behaviors of white slave owners to believe in a merciless God that *only* punishes in the face of sin? How much easier would it have been to *only* choose that version of God to emulate; to enact *only* the wrath of God and call it holy? Wielding the rod on His children for every infraction, disappointment, or perceived slight for fear they would be spoiled? How easy would it have been to reenact the brutality (at home and at church) that was heaped on black bodies and call it godly? How easy would it have been to fall in line with this behavior when you knew that at any moment, you were being watched? It would be very easy.

Hopefully, by this point, it should be clear that having been policed so heavily, in many instances the Black Church, in turn, took to policing, controlling, and sometimes abusing congregations within the confines of the church - under the pretense of holiness while largely missing holiness. This is not unusual. One of the side effects and trauma responses of being abused and controlled is the propensity to abuse and control others. It's a seed that was planted and watered. It makes the once-abused feel powerful or even justified - but it doesn't make it right.

It's All About Power

When your church is policed, you police. When you think the power of God is reduced to how He punishes, you show no mercy. The man with the microphone on Sunday morning has the power, and thus, exerts his power over others. That man polices everyone. In some denominations, a woman is not allowed by men to preach or be a part of clergy. A big part of maintaining power is keeping it out of reach from others.

Women are not exempt from the charge of having perpetuated systems of abuse and control or power trips. They, too, have sought or abused power in the church under the guise of holiness. Sometimes, their participation is outright. Other times, it is in being silent because they receive favor for "loyalty." It happens in most hierarchies. That doesn't mean it's right or that it is going to be sustainable in the Black Church for that much longer either - especially once we see more and more believers get healed and freed from oppressive theologies, get a better understanding of the inner work of holiness, and rebuke the outer focus of holiness that is weaponized to control others. We can no longer tolerate the "tradition" of the church that allows for broken people to wield power; fueling the perversion and further corrupting the generations to come.

Understanding The Search for Power

Power is not only sought by leadership. It is a strong desire for the layperson, as well. When one is stripped of power, and thus self-respect, the need for dignity, to be seen and heard, and even the ability to govern/self-govern, is sought elsewhere. The church has historically been the place where it could be found.

First, the power of God draws us in. Subconsciously, many theorize that there must be something greater than ourselves that can change things. Others know for certain that this is true. The rest just move with the crowd.

At church, we pray with the hope that we would experience the power of God to change things: the systems of oppression that result in racism, sexism, classism, and all forms of discrimination that keep one bound, in sin, and out of purpose. The prayers on a more personal scale still require God's power to heal, help a child on a destructive path, and His providence in our lives to show up in material ways.

Another kind of power that is sought is more temporal. Within the Black Church, especially following slavery, there was a power that black people could achieve that had not always been achievable in the world - even with education. Outside the church, a man could do a simple (and honest) job where he'd be unseen. And if by chance, he was seen, he was not heard. He'd have been a servant, a workhorse, a field or factory worker, a means to an end for a white establishment. Some of those who were not educated or entrepreneurial, would feel powerless to change their position. But even if a man were a sharecropper as a freedman or if a woman was a maid - at church, he is Minister Boaz. She is Minister Ruth - if that's allowed. He has a title. She has a rank. Each has "power." The ushers and deacons become "somebody." While jobs and professional opportunities have expanded to include more of us and have allowed many to attain positions of power or even simply the ability to be seen as valued for our contribution, it does not change the power structure that is still in place and revered at many churches - for the glorification of a man, and sometimes at the expense of the sheep.

Some may ask, *What's wrong with having power? It's only in the place of power that one can make decisions, change laws and policy, right?* Yes. In fact, African-Americans came together within the church to create programs and schools, battle white supremacy, and create awareness amongst one another for the sake of changing policies. During the Civil Rights Movement, the tradition of mobilizing and enacting change through the church continued. This was, indeed, good. It answered needs.

Here is where the problem of power infiltrates and corrupts the church: If the search for power is not, first and foremost, for the transformational power of Christ, the church (even those outside the black sphere) begins to over focus on hierarchies and titles, rules to control others, traditions but not a relationship with Christ, and thus, institutes churchiness over holiness where the title is more important than fulfilling the mandate that comes with the role.

When churchiness takes precedence over holiness, sectarianism (separation by sect or denomination) and doctrine police the outer "evidence" of holiness unrelated to the fruit of the Spirit and reinforce many of the oppressive tactics and cruelties we were faced with during slavery and Jim Crow.

While some churches are turning away from more stringent rules and codes, others are not. As leaders and congregants, it's time to gauge what's important by asking these questions:
- *Are we offering church? Or are we offering Jesus?*

- *Are we exhibiting holiness or churchiness?*
- *Have we been transformed?*
- *As a leader, has there been a shift in the lives of my congregants? Or are they in the same predicament and patterns for the last twenty years?*
- *Do their children keep coming when they have a choice? Might leadership have been the cause?*

These are the hard questions that church leaders must face. Dominion is not given to us to subjugate our brothers and sisters. That's domination. Dominion, however, is given for us to lead as Christ led; to steward the people well.

The early Black Church inadvertently mimicked the corrupted model of oppressing and policing black lives, partly for their own safety and because there was no other model, and in turn policed and controlled one another while presenting the appearance of holiness. At the same time, the Black Church was responsible for leading calls for social equality, integration and justice - which we must still fight for today.

We've gotten to a point where we are seeing some parts of history attempting to repeat itself. We need to be a healthy church, opposed to oppression of all kinds, abuse of all kinds, lies of all kinds. It starts in the house first. We must be a church who serves and advocates for diversity, equity, inclusion and justice for all - including the marginalized and oppressed. More than ever before, holiness will be required to navigate a new normal. Churchiness simply will not do.

III. The Tradition of Churchiness: An Enemy of Holiness

☙

Churchiness is a Preference

W E'VE GONE THROUGH A BRIEF OVERVIEW of the history of the Black Church from slavery through Jim Crow and its impact and influence. Now, for the sake of clarity, and in defense of some churchiness, some churchiness comes about because a person has been raised that way. The family church has a personality. They dance like David. They have a world class or local choir with sparkling robes. They "shout" and run in the aisle. They sing like the seraphim: *Holy, holy, holy!* It's big, it's loud, and it's exciting. There's nothing wrong with that. If it is unto God, this worship is holy. But if one grows up in this environment or their first church experience begins here, the familiarity leads one to believe that this is the only way.

Then there are those who came up in a Catholic or Anglican Church where churchiness is more quiet and "refined" worship. The choir sings in a falsetto. There are barely any stray amens except for what's part of the script. If it is unto the Lord, this worship is holy, too. Because clarity of holiness is the aim, let's be clear that the act of worship of our God is, in itself, holy. It is an inner and outer expression of praise for the Triune God. But the manner in which one worships is not the evidence of holiness. To a person growing up in either of the extremes, the other may be ridiculous or boring when compared. It is also entirely possible to enjoy, or at the very least, accept the variety because worship exalts God. Again, it comes down to preferences. Again, preferences are not the mark of holiness.

Exciting vs. Sound Preaching

The danger of only being tuned in to "exciting" church or your "solemn" preference, is that performative holiness can become the standard that determines your interest. Imagine there are two ministers at your new church. The first minister is exciting and charismatic, but uses the scripture out of context. The second minister comes to the pulpit with solid exegesis, but simple execution. Which will you choose?

The wrong choice hinders the people and keeps them in bondage. Remember the earlier description of how the enslaved people were taught about Christianity? Scripture taken out of context corrupts and keeps the people bound while exercising other rules that aim to project holiness without including the Holy Spirit in the discussion.

Don't misunderstand what's being said. There is sound preaching that is exciting. And there is sound preaching that is solemn. The thing is, exciting or solemn is not the measure of holiness.

When dance and choir and shouting and whooping and clothing choices become the standard of holiness, things get cloudy. When the quiet and solemn voice and a Eurocentric singing style becomes the standard of holiness, things get cloudy. With excitement, church can become a form of entertainment rather than reverence and praise of God and we miss the internally transformative move of God it was intended to be. With solemnity and hushed speech as the marker of holiness, church can become a starchy box that chafes and limits.

No matter the form, worship should take the focus off of us and put it in its rightful place: on God. In Luke 1:46-47 (NKJV), Mary says, *"My soul magnifies the Lord and my spirit has rejoiced in God my Savior."*

That is holiness. When the focus is on God, however it comes, holiness is abound. The Black Church can no longer church how it used to, simply relying on churchy sayings scripted worship, control and manipulation, and such. Churchiness will be the death of it, leaving grandmas and toddlers as the sole attendants.

But in holiness, there is life.

The Dangers of Churchiness

MAYBE YOU'RE WONDERING AT THIS POINT if churchiness is really that bad. Yeah, we have customs, but so what? That's our heritage. Let's take a look at the dangers.

1. Churchiness hurts the church.
Churchiness hurts the church, but it's not in the way that you think. Some churchiness is just preferred worship like we discussed in the last chapter, or it's the use of certain phrases. That's not an indictment. Churchiness, as mentioned before, has the appearance of holiness. So while it seems to focus on holy things, it can entirely miss the Holy One. It focuses on the rules and rituals of the church, rather than the move of God. The church doctrine is central to the faith but is not centered on being made like Christ. It's where denominations adopt an air of superiority that creates division. We are called to be holy and set apart, not divided as a body. Should we denounce or break away from denominations? Historically, the difference

in denominations is which part of the gospel a group found to be more important - baptism, the charismatic gifts, the sacraments and/or who they choose to oppress. [Note: It is not wrong to visit other congregations to learn different aspects of the God experience while understanding the difference is mostly in presentation and doctrinal belief.]

But should we break away from denominations? The Bible says that it creates division, so we'd be in error not to. (1 Cor. 10-17) Division hurts the church and deceives. The Baptist, for example, is not the only denomination getting into heaven, neither are they getting to heaven any faster than the Calvinist, COGIC, or Catholic. Do not be deceived into repeating these lies. Likewise, none of those faith groups are getting to heaven faster than the Baptist. Paul warns of the disunity that occurs when we make divisions amongst one another.

> *10 I urge you, brothers and sisters,[a] by the name of our Lord Jesus Christ, to agree together,[b] to end your divisions,[c] and to be united by the same mind and purpose.[d] 11 For members of Chloe's household have made it clear to me, my brothers and sisters,[e] that there are quarrels[f] among you. 12 Now I mean this, that[g] each of you is saying, "I am with Paul," or "I am with Apollos," or "I am with Cephas,"[h] or "I am with Christ." 13 Is Christ divided? Paul wasn't crucified for you, was he?[i] Or were you in fact baptized in the name of Paul?[j]* (1 Corinthians 1:10-13 NIV)

Churchiness hurts the church because it divides it. Christ is not divided. He was crucified for us.

2. Churchiness sidelines the Main Character

With churchiness, the rules of the church are central to what it means to be a Christian, but no one is following Jesus. With churchiness, having the character of Jesus is not an aspiration, but the laws and rules of the Old and New Testament are arbitrarily chosen to subjugate. The Holy Spirit is not allowed to have "main character energy" with the Father and Son, but instead plays a supporting character to our agendas, if not completely written out of the production. It's in this place that churchiness makes room for *"the false apostle, the deceitful workers, transforming themselves into apostles of Christ. And no wonder! For Satan himself transforms himself into an angel of light. Therefore, it is no great thing if his ministers transform themselves into ministers of righteousness, whose end will be according to their works."* (2 Cor. 11:13-15, NKJV)

Without yielding to the Holy Spirit we are incapable of embodying or properly identifying holiness, wisdom, or truth. We categorize others by what's familiar to the flesh or what's popular. It influences who we will be pastored by, vote for, or emulate; all of which have nothing to do with holiness.

> *"But the Lord said to Samuel, "Do not look at his appearance or at the height of his stature, because I have rejected him. For the Lord sees not as man sees; for man looks at the outward*

appearance, but the Lord looks at the heart." (1 Samuel 16:7, AMP)

3. Churchiness interferes with identifying true transformation

Let's revisit 2 Corinthians 11:13. It is important to note that the word "transform" used with the false apostle and deceitful worker is *metaschematizo*. It means to transfigure or disguise; to transform oneself into someone, to assume one's appearance. The word *metaschematizo* used in transforming themselves is the same "transform" used to describe Satan *"transforming himself as an angel of light."* This transformation implies hiding one's true identity. This is the danger of churchiness or church without the Holy Spirit. But when Romans 12:2 talks about being *"transformed by the renewing of the mind,"* it is the word *metamorphoo*. When caterpillars transform into butterflies, it's considered a metamorphosis. Similarly, this transformation means to change into another form, to transfigure the way Christ's appearance was changed and was resplendent with divine brightness. It is the appearance of the true Light of the World.

Quite obviously, the falsehood of the leadership is a danger to the church because it does not operate in the Holy Spirit. The Holy Spirit speaks to the prophet who issues a warning or a directive from the Father. The Holy Spirit allows the message to penetrate the heart. One can be emboldened to evangelize: *"Come and see a man who told me everything I ever did!"* (Jn. 4:29) The false apostle and ministers of Satan, operating in a demonic spirit, present a likeness from the flesh, where they are worshiped, and the people's flesh is gratified. Transformation has again, not taken place.

4. Churchiness institutes the Law (of Churchiness)

Churchiness is the return to the law minus the grace. God is portrayed as one-dimensional and focused only on correcting and shaming us but not developing, sanctifying, delivering, encouraging, and making us new; into His likeness in which we were created. The churchiness of sin-and-only-sin preaching is to say that God did not lead the children of Israel out of Egypt or the wilderness. Or that he did not have mercy. Or that He did not provide. Or that He did not heal. Don't misunderstand what is being said; sin is always lurking about. This was the purpose of Jesus going to the cross. But there are so many teachings about how to live as opposed to only pointing out what not to do. We do not focus on what it truly means to love God or love our neighbor. And this hurts the church.

5. Churchiness encourages a Church of hypocrisy and betrayal

Churchiness creates an allowance of sin for some, but not others depending on who the sinner is. Holiness rejects sin at all costs, even at the expense of position or title. If a preacher, for example, is mum about his own sins and failings, but broadcasts the sins of a young church brother from the pulpit, we fail as a church. That brother has been betrayed when he was supposed to be loved by the church. Abusive pastors justify this.

As Christians, even as pastors and leaders, we forget at

times that we each have a duality that we battle against: The Spirit Self vs. The Carnal Self. The new creation in whom the Holy Spirit dwells battles against the world systems and the spirits aligned with it. The new creation can find itself in battles against the old things - some that were supposed to pass away but didn't go to the grave yet. In fact, Paul talks about the things he should not do that he still does. (Romans 7:17-20) It is not unique to us, but without giving the young brother the opportunity to privately work through his inner fight with the preacher's help, the preacher has missed an opportunity to disciple and has potentially ruined a relationship. The brother may opt out of confessing sin in the future or work harder to hide it. Furthermore, the preacher has potentially put a wedge between that brother and Christ, especially if the young man saw the preacher as Christ's representative. Holiness desires and seeks discipleship.

In John 4, there is a moment at the well when Jesus talks to the woman who has had five husbands. After her encounter with Jesus, she runs into town excitedly. Her confession is that she has met a man who knew everything she'd ever done! (Jn. 4:29)

Notice the way in which Christ introduces His knowledge of her personal life. It is presented in the midst of a personal conversation in which He neither berates her publicly or privately. Instead he asks her to bring her husband. (Jn. 4:16) One interpretation of the scripture could mean He opened the door for her to be forthright, which is freedom. At that point she says that she does not have one. (Jn. 4:17) We, as readers, learn that there is no need to hide or be evasive. He already knows! It's through their private conversation that we learn, she has no husband, but has had five. And perhaps one lined up. (Jn. 4:18) At no point was it broadcast to everyone within earshot. In fact, His disciples remained at a distance and were not aware of the topic of their conversation.

6. Churchiness Covers Abuse

Churchiness covers abuse. It makes excuses for it, hides it, spins it so that it does not sound quite so bad. *I embarrassed him to keep Him from going to hell.* The assistant pastors and deacons who are silent, agree it was called for. (If they don't call it out, it is agreement.) They convince the offended that what happened wasn't so bad. They are encouraging abuse. At this level, it is bad, but excused abuse escalates. When it involves something sexual or financial, the "tangled web" gets larger. Maybe the support staff thinks they are showing love or loyalty. After all, love, a fruit of the Spirit, covers a multitude of sins. (1 Pt. 4:8) But no.

To cover means to pardon or hide. To pardon is to *remove the offense from the record after time served*. There is a difference between covering and covering up. Love (covering) helps us to overlook offense for minor errors in judgment and correcting. Excusing and denying abuse = covering up.

Love and holiness call for repentance and hold us accountable. The approach changes when we love others the way Christ loves. We have difficult conversations when we love. We offer, even to those in leadership, prayer, an action plan, or resources to overcome: books, professional counseling, or a referral for legal representation. Maybe we pair the person with someone who has grappled with a similar situation and overcome it for discipleship. Neither leaders nor the saints can do that if either chooses, instead, to hide sin.

Jesus does not promote abuse or coverups. He chastises the holy men for their hypocrisy and abuses in Matthew 23 which we will dig into at the end of section III.

Holiness does not excuse sins. It calls everybody to examine their own hearts and hold one another accountable. There are far too many exiled from the church for speaking up. There are still too many in position despite being the abuser.

7. Churchiness forgets the power of conviction

As a church, we forget that it is not our job to convict, but the Holy Spirit brings conviction. (Jn. 16:8) When we hear our sin professed in the sermon, there is a jab in the spirit. The Holy Spirit brings acute awareness to our condition, even when we are living in the midst of it and trying to excuse or justify it. That jab, the call to wake up, is the Spirit of Truth saying this thing (the sin we are engaging in) goes against Me who dwells in you. At that point, we have a choice in turning to Him in those private moments or continuing in sin. The decision to continue in sin is disobedience - which carries curses. See Deuteronomy 28:15-68.

When we, the church, forget about the power of conviction, condemnation rises up. Those who take the road of condemnation can delay repentance or incite rebellion because it is flesh, not Spirit that condemns. Romans 8:14 says, *"If you live according to the flesh, you will die."* Jesus says in John

8:15, *"You judge according to the flesh. I judge no one. And yet, if I do judge, My judgment is true; for I am not alone, but I am with the Father who sent Me."* Jesus makes distinctions about the way man judges and His judgment.

Romans 8:7-8 says,

"The carnal mind is enmity (hostile, opposed) against God; for it is not subject to the law of God, nor indeed can be. So then those who are in the flesh cannot please God."

What we can gather from these texts is that the flesh speaks to the flesh which is rebellious by nature. And to live, speak, or judge according to the flesh is not the way of God. Romans 8:16 says *"The Spirit Himself bears witness with our spirit that we are children of God."* The Spirit speaks to the spirit man who understands conviction and repents. See how that works? Speaking from the flesh has the opposite effect than what was intended. When the preacher speaks condemnation, the enemy uses the flesh which is hostile to God in just the way it was intended: to alienate and push us away from God.

Black Church Focus: Lynching

Remember in the last chapter how we discussed the church's formation throughout slavery and Jim Crow? In those days, any perceived slight or rule breaking, whether real or contrived, was rewarded with public embarrassment, whippings, and/or lynching. When slave masters wanted to break the will of the men, there was public emasculation of men being raped by slave owners or other slaves. The women were raped in front of the men. When we talk about historical trauma, black people, whose church formation was monitored and regulated by the former slave owners and religious conventions, are still experiencing some of the after effects.

During Jim Crow, black people were free from slavery. But were they really? They were still trapped by the laws that separated them from having the same rights as their white counterparts. The prison industrial complex emerged. Laws were created to enforce drastic restrictions that incurred terrible consequences. Those consequences included jail, which included a return to forced labor or slavery for even minor infractions, public torture and public lynchings while tearing families apart. With churchiness, that lynching spirit lingers.

Lynching is not only a physical act. It is possible to kill someone's spirit or enthusiasm for God by broadcasting their sin. Or by abuse of any kind. It is possible to kill someone's hope that God can help a sinner like them. One can be embarrassed and never return to church. Did the person sin? Yes. But that gets overshadowed when one is made to be a spectacle. Shame is added on top like an ice cream scoop on top of the heat of embarrassment. It melts and makes everything it encounters sticky and dirty. Shame puts people in a prison where they hide from everyone and condemn themselves even though Christ does not.

Statistics

Barna Research Group says that 37% of Americans who do not belong to a congregation "said they avoid churches because of negative past experiences in churches or with church people."[18] Leaving the church is the remedy for those who have experienced "hurt" or harm. The other reaction, which is another form of death, is to accept the abuse because it is believed "to be for your own good."

The devil is a liar. Some accept abuse because it's all they know, but get more adept at hiding their sin to lessen the potential for more abuse and to ensure they are not on the receiving end. They watch others and many silently celebrate that it is not their sin on display. Others may possibly repent, but the grace that was withheld from them may be the same grace they withhold when it happens to someone else - and someone else's spirit is lynched.

This is what I mean by churchiness hurts the church. The body suffers and passes down the suffering that I am not sure is the same suffering that Jesus said we would face. We talk about generational curses, but traumatic life experiences get passed down through systems and institutions, too. Those institutions include the church.

This raises a question: how do we stop it?

One word: Jesus. His holiness and the example He set are the reset for our souls and the remix for our lives.

---

18   https://www.barna.com/research/millions-of-unchurched-adults-are-christians-hurt-by-churches-but-can-be-healed-if-the-pain

Holiness, Control, and Manipulation

THE TRUTH IS, WE NEED JESUS AND the Holy Spirit to come into holiness. But first, we need to relinquish control. Quenching or overriding the Holy Spirit (1 Thess. 5:19) is the equivalent of choosing our own will over God's. This is the result of denying God's power and wanting to garner power for ourselves. Power is alluring. As discussed earlier, it is attractive to those who have never had it. Satan approached Eve with an offer of power - to be like God (Gen. 3:5), but it was cloaked in deceit. Why, if they were in the Garden did they need to have God's power? They already had dominion over the earth and animals. Was that not enough? And are we not similar?

Some of us read the Bible with the intent to have power over others, to bend them to what we think is right or wrong, good or evil, with the Bible as the defense. This method doesn't come from a place of love, but from a desire to feel superior or to exert control. It answers the need for power. Having power or desiring to exert power over others are two different things. Trying to exert power, or seeking to control or manipulate someone (even using scripture) is a work of the flesh that only speaks to the flesh. Satan deceived Adam and Eve in an attempt to control them by appealing to their flesh which desired power. The enemy later tried to manipulate Jesus by appealing to his flesh.

When Satan shows up in the wilderness with an offer of power, Jesus rebuked him. (Lk. 4: 1-13, Mt, 4:1-11) It seems Jesus understood the enemy's motive and was secure in who He was. Could it be that if we were secure in The One who has given us power via the Holy Spirit, that we, too, would refuse and rebuke offers of power in exchange for compromise?

The thing is, we do have power that is gained by reading the Scripture and believing because we know the truth of who God is. God's truth is power because it thwarts the enemy's lies, schemes and plans. We also have power because the Word says *"You will have power when the Holy Spirit comes upon you."* (Acts 1:8) But power that is not fueled by the will of God and empowered by His Spirit can be perverted and used for evil - even if it has the appearance of holiness.

This quest for power is sometimes the reason those who have not been called enter religious spaces seeking leadership roles. It is how the sheep get taken advantage of. Remember, my focus is on the Black Church, some of whom may not have been delivered from the spirit of control - that infamous "Jezebel" spirit that is always (errantly) ascribed to women. With the desire for power, control and manipulation become the tools of choice. The pretense of holiness makes control and manipulation appear acceptable or warranted.

It makes holiness a control method to keep the saints in line. Can you have a doctrine for your church? Absolutely. Have a dress code or don't. Sing with music or without. That's your prerogative, but neither is that evidence of holiness.

If doctrine goes beyond creating order for the church or identifying your beliefs, core values, or credo about God, it can become a dangerous tool. When it involves shaming others, it is dangerous. It kills the spirit and fosters the idea that conformity is required to belong to the church. We are not called to conformity with one another. We are flawed humans. We are called to conform to the image of Christ (Rom. 8:29), we are called to *"be transformed by the renewing of our minds"* (Rom. 12:2) and we are called to *"keep the unity of the Spirit through the bond of peace."* (Eph. 4:3-6)

Christ is the example whose commandments call us to conform to His character. Beating a person into submission physically, verbally, or emotionally is a fear tactic that perpetuates slavery (of mind, body, or soul) or incites rebellion. So where one has not submitted to the power of the Holy Spirit and received the fruit of self-control, the same will use humanly attained power to regulate and control others.

METHODS OF CONTROL
Performative Holiness

When the pastor enters the sanctuary with a robe to the floor or a three-piece suit, it is not evidence of holiness. Those are his clothing choices or the priestly tradition of the denomination. It is not evidence of the Holy Ghost. The preacher's charisma and ability to get you stirred up is not evidence that the Holy Spirit is inspiring him. While some may weep for various reasons, eliciting emotion from the congregation is not necessarily evidence of the Holy Ghost. Clothing and performance can convince the churchgoer that the Pastor is operating in the Spirit. The presence of holiness is not reduced to one simple thing. It's his character, what comes out of his mouth, whether it aligns with scripture. It's how the preacher engages with church members and what he or she does in private. We won't know everything about the pastor, but that person would be integral; not found living a double life. When confronted with sin, the response would be as David responded to Nathan (2 Sam. 12:13), understanding that repenting immediately is mandatory. This is important because with the introduction of performative holiness, there is an unconscious response where the sheep reciprocate the performance of the shepherd. It begins in a seemingly innocent weekly church interaction. Let's look more closely.

When the pastor whoops, some of the sheep feel the need to respond by standing or clapping whether the teaching is accurate or not - but sounds good. Some will be prayed over and will fall down because they think it's expected. Some preachers will push the people and they don't want the preacher to look bad or that they didn't feel the power so they will drop. This is what sheep under the wrong shepherd do. They, too, are performative. It seems like nothing, but it's insidious because it is acting. It's even more dangerous because when it doesn't look like this, the people are confused. Those who don't "feel the power" when prayed for, begin to think God hasn't touched them. Meanwhile, the biggest question is not whether or not the show was good, but whether or not hearts are transformed.

Holy Aesthetics

We'll get into this a little more deeply in section V, but when we focus on image or a curated presentation, we create a holy aesthetic as a standard for identifying holiness, and then we exact those standards on others. *How is he a pastor if he's wearing a sweatshirt? How is First Lady supposed to teach us to be holy with red nails? Oh, I know Deacon is holy because he can quote scripture.* So does the devil. (Lk. 4:10-11)

Many entertain wolves because the wrong criteria is used in identifying them. Trying to identify whether someone else is holy by outward appearance is like looking through blurry glasses of our own perceptions and assumptions. Can one discern unclean spirits? Yes. But many don't. It's their own bias, personal taste, or projection of their own shortcomings that paint the fuzzy picture.

THE REMEDY
Self-Control & Self-Mastery Kills the Need for Forced Modesty

Cover the women's kneecaps when they sit near the front row in a dress. Sister's red lipstick is calling too much attention to her. We all know there are some women who come to church with an agenda. Just like there are men who come with an agenda. But first and foremost, dear pastors and leaders, it's on you to master yourself.

For you (and all of us) to, *"Put on the full armor of God that you may be able to stand against the wiles of the devil"* is the first step in mastering oneself. We focus too much on the "wiles of the devil" thinking it's always external. However, it's been said that the failure to control oneself leads to the desire to control others. Let that marinate.

We blame others. But guarding your heart is first a "you" job. That's the first part of dominion that is missed. God gave Adam and Eve a command, but they failed to master the dominion over themselves by following His command.

If you find yourself tempted by something you see, get in the Lord's face. Ask the Holy Spirit to take over and for the fruit of self-control to be your portion. Jesus said, *"If your eye causes you to stumble, pluck it out. It is better for you to enter the kingdom of God with one eye than to have two eyes and be thrown into hell, where the worms that eat them do not die, and the fire is not quenched."* (Mk. 9:47-48) This isn't Old Testament, this is JESUS. Holiness comes through accountability for one's own vices, thoughts, and actions. It comes through removing oneself from the situation, not in simply policing or controlling others.

In the pulpit and in the pews, men and women alike police women about appropriate attire because a dress code standard has been set. Are dress codes bad? It depends. You're not going to wear swim trunks or a wedding gown to church just as you wouldn't wear them to the supermarket or to school. They are appropriate attire for certain places and events. The issue is that as a church, we have reduced holiness to a standard that tells the women to cover up. Wear long(er) skirts. Cover your breasts. Don't wear body hugging clothing. Wear shorts and a t-shirt in the pool. No red lipstick and no red nail polish allowed. Sometimes, the young men are encouraged to wear a suit and tie. No sneakers. No sweats or joggers because of "the print."

Is this advocacy for scandalous church attire? No. But let that be a conversation and not a condemnation. Learn intention before inviting contention. We're not doing shame and calling it holiness. Besides, when the Holy Spirit begins to do the inner workings on identity (which will be discussed later) and who we belong to, outfit choices change.

Revisit the Meaning of Modesty

There is nothing wrong with asking the congregation to dress up or down. Also, there's nothing wrong with the church having a culture of modesty, but let's be clear: scriptural modesty was related to showboating and being ostentatious.

> 1 Peter 3:1-4 says,
> *Wives, likewise, be submissive to your own husbands, that even if some do not obey the word, they, without a word, may be won by the conduct of their wives, 2 when they observe your chaste conduct accompanied by fear. 3 Do*

> *not let your adornment be **merely** outward— arranging the hair, wearing gold, or putting on fine apparel— 4 rather let it be the hidden person of the heart, with the [a]incorruptible beauty of a gentle and quiet spirit, which is very precious in the sight of God.*

Context matters. So although this pertains to wives and husbands, the text is saying that your adornment should be internal as well as external (if you so please.) Since the text says, *"Do not let it be merely (simply or only) outward"* merely indicates that external is fine, but that can't be all. If we look at this being the bride of Christ, there is nothing wrong with women being beautiful before the Bridegroom. The true measure of beauty can be found in the heart. It's in the behavior and the attitude she exudes that is deemed to be the best adornment or dressing. It's the heart the Bridegroom truly desires, not merely the Bride's appearance. The Bridegroom does not shun those who adorn themselves outwardly, but He asks that the heart be the true adornment.

> 1 Timothy 2:8-10 says,
> *8 I desire therefore that the men pray everywhere, lifting up holy hands, without wrath and doubting; 9 in like manner also, that the women adorn themselves in modest apparel, with propriety and [e]moderation, not with braided hair or gold or pearls or costly cloth-*

ing, 10 but, which is proper for women professing godliness, with good works.

In the first century, the people of Israel, Rome, and Greece wore long robes or tunics. The idea of modesty had to do with showing off wealth, not tantalizing the menfolk with their clothing choices or lack of pantyhose. For the record, while they are helpful in "holding things together," pantyhose don't make you any more holy that those who don't wear them.

That means if we are policing, then Gucci bags, diamond earrings, furs, and ostentatious displays to show one's (image of having) wealth would have to go. If we're doing modesty, the hard-to-find Jordans are forbidden. Take back that Rolls-Royce Cullinan and get that Honda CRV, Sir. That is, if you really want to talk about modesty.

Understand Jesus and the Whitewashed Tombs

Furthermore, if holiness were about what you wear, remember that John the Baptist looked like a madman with his outfit choices. (Mk. 1:6) The people said he had a demon! (Mt. 11:18) But Jesus said *"of those born of a woman, none were greater than John."* (Mt. 11:11)

Remember, too, that Jesus told the Pharisees in their phylacteries, fringes, long robes and long, uncut beards that they were like whitewashed tombs. If that doesn't seem like an insult, consider this: He told men who wore "holy clothes" they were like a mausoleum; clean on the outside, but housing the rotting flesh of dead men. (Mt. 23:27)

If holiness were a matter of what you wear, all the women who wear skirts to their ankles and all-white-everything on first Sundays would only sing *holy, holy, holy* with angels in heaven. There would be no praying for the dissolution of another woman's marriage so you could have her husband, no fornication with either gender, no stealing, lying, cover ups, child abuse cases, gaslighting or ostracizing those who come forward about abuse, gossiping about the things that people come to you about for prayer, and overall meanness.

If holiness were about clothing, then all the men who wear suits and robes in the pulpit would all go to heaven, seated on God's right hand next to Jesus. There would be no scandals, scams, stealing, lying, domestic violence, adultery, backstabbing, hidden children, fornication with either gender, rape, or molestation or sexual assault of children.

Lastly, I'd like to point out that no one knew Jesus was the Messiah because He did not look like a holy man or Pharisee. He did not look like a warrior. He did not look like a king. And yet, He was the Christ.

Because we were born in iniquity, being born again and made a new creation (1 Co. 5:17) is the opportunity for us to be resurrected from death - from sin - and filled with the Holy Spirit. When we follow Him we are the light of the world and do not walk in darkness, but have the light of life. (John 8:12) When we do not follow Him, darkness prevails.

By now you must have surmised the obvious: Holiness is not simply based on the external. It is not simply in the priestly garments: the tunic, ephods, or breastplates. Neither is it simply in the sharpest Sunday suit, choir robe, or the whitest of white First Sunday usher board dress. Those are dupes that deceive us. Aaron's sons wore those things according to Levitical law, but *"offered profane fire before the Lord which He had not commanded them. So fire went out from the Lord and devoured them, and they died before the Lord."* (Leviticus 10:1-2)

Similarly, when offering profane fire before the Lord, that which He had not commanded, some may be met with a similar fate. Fire may go out from the Lord and devour you, maybe in resources, relationships, or peace of mind. I know we don't like to say this, and we know God is merciful and desires all to be saved, but you may die. We have no idea. When the day of Judgment comes, many a hardened heart in holy garb will cry out and be met with the rebuke, *"I never knew you; depart from Me, you who practice lawlessness!"* (Mt. 7:23)

Because identifying holiness is a matter of the heart, identifying holiness will require finding evidence of God in their speech and matching actions: their fruit. At the same time, we must take inventory of our own fruit. Without God who is holy, there is no holiness.

The Power of Discipleship

Many of us won't know someone's story or their "why" because rather than disciple, we ostracize and force our members to become outer holy, fake holy, performative holy.

And that's why Jesus invited the disciples to follow Him. He was teaching, listening, observing, correcting, loving, and preparing them for His departure. It's also why he berated the teachers (Mt. 23) and warned the people of wolves in sheep's clothing. (Mt. 7:15) It was for protection of the sheep.

The Spiritual Hospital with Sick Doctors

The church is the healing hospital for the sick, but some of the doctor ministers have not seen the Great Physician for themselves nor have they filled the prescriptions to correct disease. They read the manual but miss the part about surrender. The Holy Spirit is just a buzzword tossed about, but even they don't believe. So a sick doctor is operating on sick patients and all of a sudden, it's a pandemic of the Walking Dead; doing all the church things minus the holy heart. The heart is not yielded to God. It is dead to the things of God. It is the Church of Sardi, yet again. (Rev. 3:1)

A New Approach

Can we privately mention to the new young woman that her outfit will invite unwarranted attention? Sure. But she may already know and desire that. It's sticky. This is the place where discernment and prayer need to be employed heavily. If it's determined she's not on a demonic assignment, it's up to us to keep loving her, keep talking to her, and maybe teach the women (and the men, too!) about one's internal value, understanding motives of the heart, and the things that fill the heart. It is wise to teach everyone, even those who've "been there for years" because some don't know something because they have not been taught and don't even think to ask. Clothing, for women, is oftentimes an outer expression of the heart and one's perceived identity outside of Christ. Other times, they may be simply emulating the example of women they've known or a TV personality they admire.

Learning the hearts of others before imposing an external standard goes a whole lot further than requiring conformity. The Black Church, like some others, was birthed through stringent rules and oppression that required conformity. God doesn't ask for conformity, people do. God transforms the heart if we let Him. The transformed heart surrenders to the leading of the Holy Spirit and gains discernment for one's own behavior and the dangers lurking. Holiness is an internal job. It starts from the inside - with a pure heart; a cleansed heart that is renewed daily.

When the scripture says, *"Beloved, I pray that you may prosper in all things and be in health, just as your soul prospers,"* it's not hard to imagine that the soul prospers when the heart is pure, filled with the beauty of holiness.

This is the desire, not just for leadership, but for all followers of Christ.

None of us have seen all there is to see in life. But it is less likely that we will ever see a person's life turned around because their pastor preached well and whooped and danced, but lived an unholy, unsurrendered, un-set apart life.

In fact, Jesus warned the holy men about this kind of folly. Let's take a look at what He had to say.

Jesus & The Churchy Holy Men

Now, we are very clear that Jesus expressed mercy and grace for the people he encountered. If He spoke about things that needed correction, it was often in group settings. He seemed to avoid singling anyone out and making a spectacle of them - except when it came to reprimanding the Holy Men of His time. Did you ever notice, however, that the people that Jesus publicly called out were the leaders: the Pharisees who would have been considered holy? Matthew 23 is an assassination of the churchiness of the Pharisees who *performed holiness* at a high standard. Let's take a look at a few verses:

> *1 Then Jesus said to the crowds and to his disciples, 2 "The scribes and the Pharisees sit on Moses' seat, 3 so do and observe whatever they tell you, but not the works they do. For they preach, but do not practice. 4 They tie up heavy burdens, hard to bear,[a] and lay them*

on people's shoulders, but they themselves are not willing to move them with their finger. 5 They do all their deeds to be seen by others. For they make their phylacteries broad and their fringes long, 6 and they love the place of honor at feasts and the best seats in the synagogues 7 and greetings in the marketplaces and being called rabbi[b] by others. 8 But you are not to be called rabbi, for you have one teacher, and you are all brothers.[c] 9 And call no man your father on earth, for you have one Father, who is in heaven. 10 Neither be called instructors, for you have one instructor, the Christ. 11 The greatest among you shall be your servant. 12 Whoever exalts himself will be humbled, and whoever humbles himself will be exalted. 13 "But woe to you, scribes and Pharisees, hypocrites! For you shut up the kingdom of heaven against men; for you neither go in [yourselves], nor do you allow those who are entering to go in. 14 "Woe to you, scribes and Pharisees, hypocrites! For you devour widows' houses, and for a pretense make long prayers. Therefore you will receive greater condemnation. 15 "Woe to you, scribes and Pharisees, hypocrites! For you travel land and sea to win one proselyte, and when he is won, you make him twice as much a son of hell as yourselves. ... 27 "Woe to you, scribes and Pharisees, hypocrites! For you are like whitewashed tombs which indeed appear beautiful outwardly, but inside are full of dead [men's] bones and all uncleanness. (Matthew 23:1-15, 27, ESV)

Jesus's reproach was scathing! What was He saying then and now?[19]

He first advised His disciples and the multitude, those listening to His sermon in the presence of the Pharisees, that the Pharisees do have authority, so it was acceptable to observe the teachings. A little research uncovered the fact that the "synagogues had a seat that the authoritative teacher sat,"[20] which they called Moses' seat. (Mt. 23:2-3) For Jesus to say they sit in the seat of Moses is to say that as Moses relayed God's word and law, so do the Pharisees. Right after that He calls them hypocrites, those who preach one thing but do another. *Bang!* (Mt. 23:3)

The first warning shot was fired. Its aim was to differentiate Jewish churchiness from holiness and pretense from good character. He warns those within the sound of His voice to follow the teaching but not the behaviors of the Pharisees.

Then he fires a machine gun of rebukes against them.

He tells them that these teachers are going to ask the impossible of you while they themselves do the minimum, if anything at all. *Bang!* (Mt. 23:4)

---

19   If you have your Bible open, it will make this interpretation smoother and you can makes notes.
20   David Guzik Commentary/Study Guide for Matthew 23.

They do good in front of others so that they can be applauded and praised by men. *Bang!* (Mt. 23:5)

They wear holy clothing to be seen. *Bang!* (Mt. 23:5)

They desire front row seats. *Bang!* (Mt. 23:6)

And favor. *Bang!* (Mt. 23:6)

And titles. *Bang!* (Mt. 23:7)

Does that sound like those who want the likes and follows of today? There's nothing new under the sun. Jesus warns His disciples not to do these things; to not be called Father or Teacher because we are all brothers and sisters in the faith. This was a rebuke of those who desired titles for reasons of self-importance and pretentiousness. *Bang, bang, bang!* (Mt. 23:8-9)

Jesus, for lack of a better term, chose violence throughout this chapter.

A Spiritual Massacre

Remember we talked about killing or lynching not only being a physical act of ending a life in the previous section, Jesus rolled through these verses aiming the sword at ambition, pride, and error in which the Pharisees were operating. He was killing the misconceptions of the kingdom of God and lynching the oppressive religious system that would in fact keep the people from ever attaining entrance both in their present day and in eternity. Jesus points the saints toward Himself as the example of the servant. He told the multitude that the Pharisees were not getting to God and made it impossible for men to get to God. (Mt. 23:12-13)

The Pharisees who should be shepherds and intercessors, the connect to God, had become obstacles to the maturity and growth of the sheep, and an obstacle even to the voice of God. (Mt. 23:13) The Pharisees are like the preachers who say that only they hear from God while even those who are not in "official" service to God have also been given the gift.

The Final Sweep

Jesus went on to say that they take advantage of the widows in the congregation. (Mt. 23:14)

In His culture, widows were unprotected in society and, thus, vulnerable. Devouring their houses could mean overtaking their finances and resources and even their bodies. These kinds of "priests" pray long prayers for show. The long prayers appear to be pious, but they are a snare.

Jesus then says that the leader/mentor gets one person to follow him, but because he doesn't follow God, neither does the mentee. In fact, he becomes worse than the teacher. (Mt. 23:15) If we put this in perspective, we can see that the mentor's behavior can be become a justification for the mentee. *If my mentor does it, then it can't be wrong.* Or they may understand it's wrong, but when presented with an opportunity says, *If he can, I can.*

Jesus says the holy men, though they appear to look clean or pure, become an eternal prison to the men whose spirit they've killed with all the regulations and with their own sins that lead humanity astray. (Mt. 23:27) Jesus warns

against these things because He cares for the sheep.
Matthew 23:16-26 contains even more rebukes. Every rebuke on the page is there to cause the leaders to repent. As we read, it is a warning of what not to be and what to look out for. That Jesus addressed this means that we are each responsible for how we behave and what we condone.

Why Rebuke Matters for Leaders

Reader, if you are not already, you will at some point be a leader. And when you are a leader, you will not always get it right. There will be a rebuke. And sometimes, the rebuke won't always be a one-on-one moment. Take heart.

When Jesus says, *"Get thee behind me, Satan"* as a rebuke to Peter, it is both a public and private moment because Peter is rebuked amongst the other Disciples, but it is not the one-on-one interaction we'd previously seen or would prefer. In Peter's defense, he meant well. But he was speaking about a spiritual matter with a carnal mind. (Mk. 8:33, Mt. 16:23) Similarly, Paul (the former Pharisee) publicly embarrassed Peter for allowing certain behaviors until the other apostles arrived. (Gal. 2:11-14) Leadership was not exempt from correction back then. Even though it seems like they are, neither are they exempt now.

To be a teacher was to have greater responsibility and to be held to a higher standard because they could cause one of His children to stumble. Matthew 18:7 says, *"Woe to the world because of the things that cause people to stumble! Such things must come, but woe to the person through whom they come!"* Jesus was not speaking of teachers at this moment, but how much more of a responsibility does a teacher have than those who are unaware?

Mishandling the sheep through churchiness rather than Christ's example is to cause the children to stumble. One mishandles the sheep by abusing one's title and stature, by taking advantage of the vulnerable, by keeping God away from the people, by holding one standard in public and another in private. The mishandling occurs when being exact on the law even for minor infractions, but failing to disclose one's own failings or remembering the mercy that God shows.

For leadership to deny love, truth, integrity, and thus mercy to those they shepherd is to quench or put out the fire of the Holy Spirit. Without the Holy Spirit, can holiness abound? And does it matter?

IV. Why Holiness Matters

IV / Why Hotness Matters

Holiness & the Holy Spirit

HOLINESS IS A HEART MATTER. The reason holiness matters is because it is a state of being where we are most closely aligned with God and resemble Him. This is where we are living a sanctified and mature life; where the level of access we give to the Holy Spirit is evident.

Holiness, if you haven't discerned, is a lifestyle influenced by the Holy Spirit (the Spirit of God). Our thoughts and actions are influenced by the Holy Spirit and God's will is done. This is why monitoring the outer things can be futile.

That Holy Spirit-influenced lifestyle produces the beautiful spiritual fruit that is the indication of a pure heart. What does that mean? There are things we read in the Scripture, like the Ten Commandments, for example. We know those are the rules. And then there is Jesus explaining that when He leaves, He will send a Helper. When we accept Jesus as Lord and Savior, we receive the Helper, the Holy Spirit. The Holy Spirit lives inside us to help us so that our hearts are inclined to obey the commandments, for example.

Will we always do the right thing once we receive the Holy Spirit? No. Help only works if accepted. If we don't accept the Helper that is the Holy Spirit, we lean to the desires of the flesh and it becomes easier to miss the mark. Because we have the option of whether or not to allow help, there can be degrees to how much (if any) access is given for the Spirit to operate and the fruit that is produced.

How? Because we put boundaries on the Holy Spirit. Inwardly, we say, *I listen to You here, but not there. I allow You into this section of my life, but not that one.* For example, we may listen to the Holy Spirit when instructed to apologize. But maybe not when He says to let go of that "romance."

What we idolize is often revealed in this place. Maybe you don't idolize being right. But continuing the relationship may be an indication that you have idolized marriage or maybe you've idolized your own intellect or your own desires.

The byproduct of giving the Holy Spirit reign over your life is holiness - set apart for God's use. Holiness does not necessarily indicate ease. Holiness calls us to consecration. It removes what is not for us both inside and out.

At the same time, holiness gives us discernment. Charles Spurgeon said, "Discernment is not knowing the difference between right and wrong. It is knowing the difference between right and almost right." When God says, "That ain't it. Let it go," in obedience, we let go.

Obedience is a sign of holiness because Jesus obeyed the Father. If Jesus was obedient and He is holy, then our obedience indicates holiness.

The Upside to Holiness

Now let's get this out there: Even in holiness, even when you have surrendered to the Holy Spirit and given full access, you still have a personality, quick wit, humor, or dramatic demeanor, for example. You will still be passionate about the projects you take on, but the scope of the projects may change. In this place, purpose can be discovered. But the need to appear holy to fit into your church group becomes a thing of the past. It's no longer about the image of holiness, but actual holiness. Although there are some uncomfortable moments, there are beautiful upsides to holiness.

1. ***Your choices become Holy Spirit inspired!*** What you will wear, who you will befriend, remain friends with, or no longer keep in contact with will be reviewed.

Content you will create, books or film you may write, where you will go or not go, where you will worship, whose teaching you will listen to, who you will consider for marriage, remain married to, or leave, will be influenced by God, not world standards and not the image you desire to portray for acceptance.

2. **Power.** Jesus told the Apostles, *"You will receive power when the Holy Spirit comes upon you."* (Acts 1:8) Maybe we think power is some sparkly, tingly feeling on the inside, where we sprout wings on the outside. But after Pentecost, the men were able to speak in the tongues of others. (Acts 2:6-12) The ability to communicate is Holy Spirit power! The ability for someone else to receive what you've shared is Holy Spirit power!

3. **_Transformation and Maturity._** God is in the business of transformation. He meets you at the well, just as you are, but He desires you to grow. It is entirely possible for many saints to grow in age, but remain mentally, emotionally, and spiritually immature. God does not desire that we remain drinking milk in any aspect of our lives - hence the gift of the Holy Spirit.

Spiritual immaturity will have you praying and seeing no progress in your life, no revelation, no reconciliation in your families, no ending to generational curses or trauma, no healing and no understanding of the things of God - including holiness.

The Holy Spirit within you cultivates and encourages holiness. It is the source of that transformation and the maturity or sanctification of our hearts. Sanctification means maturation which means we are growing up to be more like Christ which is the end game. Immaturity, then, is remaining unchanged; stagnant internally, even if outer things change. The Holy Spirit partners with us in our prayers (Romans 8:26) and builds up our faith when we pray in the Holy Spirit. (Jude 20) We need that faith because *"without faith it is impossible to please God, because anyone who comes to Him must believe that He exists and that He rewards those who diligently seek Him."* (Heb. 11:6) Could that mean then that there is no holiness without faith?

When you block out the sound of God's voice or the nudging or pull of the Spirit, you begin to drift away from holy. The Fruit of the Spirit is choked out by the fruit of the flesh. The pure heart becomes the polluted heart. The reprobate mind is sure to follow. (Rm. 1:28)

But God. God desires holiness. That is the number one reason why holiness matters. It's in this desire that His will be done in us and in the Kingdom. It is because of this desire that He gives us the gift of repentance so that we are never too far away from Him.

And finally, with this understanding of why it matters, let us get into the re-introduction to holiness and what it looks like.

V. The Re-Introduction to Holiness

In All Things Get Understanding of God

To GET AN UNDERSTANDING OF HOLINESS, we will need to get the clearest possible understanding of who God is and what makes God holy.

How do we do that? By digging into the Bible, observing how He interacts with creation, Adam and Eve, the patriarchs, Moses, the Israelites, the judges and kings, the prophets, the disciples and followers, the women, the crowds, and the Pharisees, for example. Every time we notice something, we make notes. We compile evidence of God's attributes, actions, and desires for us with the same energy used to find intel before a first date. Think of it as building a dossier on God with things like His names and aliases, where He resides or His location, goals, requirements, pet peeves, miracles, character, and attributes; things like that.

Now, sometimes, God's attributes are hidden in the names He is given. Sometimes His attributes can be located in the things He does, what pleases Him and what does not. Have you considered that because God desires that you have life and have it more abundantly (John 10:10) means He is generous or thoughtful? Some things are not spelled out, but inferred. It's dossier material. We can use it as a measuring stick for holiness - starting first with our own.

After investigation, we can also get the understanding of who God is by revelation. God can be revealed to us even as it was revealed to Peter when Jesus asked *"Who do you say that I Am?"* Peter identified Jesus as the Christ which was a revelation from God. (Mt. 16:14-17)

Let's be clear: our human understanding has limitations. However, the aim is to gather as much intel as possible about God's character; not simply the rules to follow or laud over others. We desire to learn more about His character because His character determines ours. Oftentimes, we can overlook the character of someone we know because they perform in a certain role. For us, that person is our protector and we don't seek to understand that person outside of that role. In the same way, it is entirely possible to read the Bible cover to cover and fail to discover the character of God because we are focused on the wrong things. Without at least a baseline understanding of who He is and what His character looks like, it is, and always will be impossible to define holiness or how we might embody it.

With that being said, because we may never be able to encapsulate the fullness of God, defining holiness might be just as much of a task. The limitation is not that we are not smart. The limitation exists because defining holiness, despite a high IQ, is restricted by our limitations of what "makes sense" to us as human beings. Many of us, for example, believe sexuality and nudity to be unholy when in fact they are holy. Have they been perverted in many ways? Yes. But it doesn't change the idea that holiness can be found in sexuality and nudity. Many marriages are flailing and failing because of a misunderstanding of holiness and sexuality. But that's a book by a different author.

We can miss out on identifying the holy in other areas of life, as well, because we have a rigid definition of a holiness that may not be scriptural but churchfluenced. By churchfluenced, I mean churchiness or tradition-based influence. Because holiness has been misconstrued as an outward posture by many, instead of recognizing maturity in ourselves and others, it has been used as a construct to control others under the guise of presenting an *image* of spiritual purity.

But what does that mean?

The Image of Spiritual Purity

In Genesis 1:27, God created us in His image and likeness. That means that when God created us, we resembled Him spiritually by His design and were to rule as He does - but we are not God. Though we are not God, God calls us, even after the fall of Adam and Eve, to be holy. In Leviticus 20:26, Moses speaks God's command to the children of Israel, namely the priests - which is all of us (1Pet. 2:9). He says, *"You shall be holy to Me, for I the Lord am holy, and have separated you from the peoples, that you should be Mine."* This command comes after a series of behaviors that He encourages or condemns starting with offerings (Lev. 1-7), consecration, conduct, and punishment of the priests (Lev. 8-10) and then laws.

At this point in the scripture, God is preparing them to go into the land of milk and honey, the nation whose statutes they must absolutely not follow, but whose territory they will possess. There, they will need discernment between clean and unclean behaviors, as well as, clean and unclean birds, animals, and creeping things. (Lev. 20:2-25) God is changing the patterns they've learned over centuries of enslavement for the sake of developing internal discipline. This way they will mature and remain holy - spiritually in tune with Him - wherever they go. This is our call as well.

While He calls us to be holy, to resemble Him spiritually, oftentimes, the church's idea of holy may bypass the inner resemblance for the public image or outer resemblance that can be more easily identified. The image is the public reputation/presentation that has been crafted to intentionally resemble what one thinks is acceptable, popular, or in line with the church culture to which they belong. That resemblance of holiness (that which is not actually holiness) is the image of spiritual purity. It seeps out into regular life, but backfires in so many ways.

Let's say you're a Christian organization looking for a spokesperson to lead the young people back to holiness. You have narrowed down the search to two applicants. You go to one girl's social media account to learn more of who she is. Her page is filled with pics of her wearing a cross, big t-shirts and baggy jeans while giving clothes to the homeless. She also posts videos and memes about being kind. She has pics at the very popular church she attends. Unbeknownst to you, she stages the giveaways, gives only a portion of what she claims to, and only helps if recipients agree to be photographed. That is someone who has crafted an external image in an effort to gain social proof. She presents the image of spiritual purity. Her spiritual purity is like AI. She looks flawless even though the picture is not quite her.

The young woman presented an "image" to control how others perceived her. If she is perceived in the way she would like, she is favored. She is hired. She becomes the face of the organization whose hiring manager, without the aid of the Holy Spirit, wrongly chooses her over the genuine candidate who may not be as polished, but has great references. We cannot see the choice is corrupt unless or until she is exposed as a fraud. That's how it looks on the layperson.

When pastors and church leaders operate from the image of spiritual purity over actual spiritual purity, the consequences are more dire. The image attempts to wrangle control away from God and deceives.

If, for example, you believe "Pastor" is a certain way based on what he intentionally presents and preaches to you, but he is not that person, he is deceiving you.

Why deceive you? First, he is deceived, himself. After that, there are many possibilities. For some, though it may have begun that way, it is no longer about winning souls to Christ, but filling up the seats in his church and expanding.

There is power in having a large church. And power is addictive. But some forget that the power we truly want is the power of the Holy Spirit to transform. The deceit is about controlling you and your fellow congregants by presenting an image - even if the image is one of power.

Because there is an exchange in some power-fueled relationships, in turn, some saints present an image to belong to the organization. They fawn over the Pastor, defer to him as the authority of things they are fully capable of deciding in counsel with God, and revere him. We discussed in a previous chapter, the people who perform churchy behaviors. It's the same pattern.

For many churchgoers, it's all a part of belonging. There's nothing wrong with belonging. But it's entirely possible to belong to a church but not to Christ and absolutely nothing changes internally. Holiness is not present and scripture tells us why. In Matthew 15 (NIV), the Pharisees and teachers of the law come to Jesus to call out the disciples for not washing their hands. Jesus rebukes them. Not only does He rebuke them, Jesus recites Isaiah's prophecy, *"These people honor me with their lips but their hearts are far from me. They worship me in vain, their teachings are merely human rules."* (Mt.15:8, Is. 29:13)

In reciting the scripture to them, He points out that in all their own study of Isaiah, they missed the mark. If your heart is far from God, but you proclaim the rules loudly, you're missing the mark, too. Let's delve into God's identity so we can examine the blueprint of holiness.

God's Identity
Who God is: God the Father

> *"Then Moses said to God, "Indeed when I come to the children of Israel and say to them, "The God of your fathers has sent me to you, and they say to me what is His name?" what shall I say to them?" And God said to Moses, "I AM WHO I AM." And He said, "Thus you shall say to the children of Israel, "I AM has sent me to you."* (Ex. 3:13-14, NKJV)

Moses was thrust into the assignment of leading the children of Israel out of Egypt. He would need God for every step of the journey. But who was this God? He likely wondered, *How in the world do I explain the name of the God of their fathers?* Today, we have a list of names from which we could choose. But for Moses, which one name would suffice?

Not only did Moses seek to clarify God's identity, but Moses needed to know in whose authority he was going. So when Moses asked, the NKJV translation reports that God said, "I AM has sent me to you." Other translations say, "I AM who I AM." or "I Am That I Am." And one says, "I Will Be What I Will Be." All express that God is the God of yesterday, today, and forever. In other words, as God of their fathers, God wanted them (and us) to know: I Was, I Am, I Will Be.

God's response of "I Am" aids in our understanding that God, right now today, encompasses every aspect of goodness - even beyond our capacity to understand goodness.

"I Am" is God speaking of Himself and the innumerable attributes of His Divinity. Let's dig further into God's identity and character by observing His actions in Genesis. If we are to be holy, we must learn who the Holy God is so that we, too, can identify holiness and model what's been shown.

Understanding God's Identity

Genesis 1

God is the Creator.

The scripture starts off, *"In the beginning, God created the heavens and the earth."* If what God does is who He is then He is the Creator. But to the children of Israel, it may not have been an adequate way to express who'd sent Moses. However, He is God whose creation begins first with the Ruach Elohim (Gen. 1:2), the breath of God, with the stamp of His image and likeness (Gen. 1:27), with the ability to recreate, and to have dominion over all things (Gen. 1:26,28) including seed-bearing plants and trees and the animals of land and sea that reproduce. (Gen. 1:29) Naturally, His children also carry and birth children from seed - being fruitful and multiplying. (Gen. 1:28) Beyond bearing children from seed, the ideas He gives are the seed to be able to create.

God the Father is the Creator because He creates image bearers who create.

Genesis 4

God is Just, Protective, and Merciful.

When Cain, the wayward child of Adam and Eve murdered his brother in the field (Gen. 4:8), he was afraid that he would be killed by those who knew of his wrongdoing. (Gen. 4:14) So while he was cursed to work hard with no reward and be a vagabond (Gen. 4:12) for that terrible act, God also branded him with a mark. (Gen. 4:15) The mark made those who knew of his deed aware that Cain belonged to God and could not be touched.

God the Father executes justice because He is Justice, thus, Cain was exiled for his sin. Fathers execute justice as a way to discipline us. God the Father protects because He is the Protector. Cain was branded with a mark that meant he was protected. God the Father exhibits mercy because He is mercy. Cain was spared and went on to father children and build a city. (Gen. 4:16-17)

Genesis 6
God is Judgment.

Judgment is the weighing of your activity with either warning, course correction, or punishment. We see this first with Adam and Eve, and then in the story of Cain. With the entry of sin, there was a detour from God's initial intentions. Adam and Eve's disobedience separated them and thus their descendants from the holiness in which they were created. They had one job: obey the command to stay away from the tree of good and evil. (Gen. 3:3) Now, were they deceived? Yes. However, they made a decision. God is many things, but He is not a puppet master. He established that when He gave them dominion. Dominion starts first with ruling over ourselves, making the proper decisions. Holiness comes from making decisions with Him in mind - which they did not do. Their choices determined the direction in which they went and thus, the judgment.

Despite what we've been terrorized into believing, it is not God's intention to strike down every wrongdoing. None of us would be here. But there came a time when He said, *"My Spirit shall not strive with man forever, for he is indeed flesh; yet his days shall be one hundred twenty years."* (Gen. 6:3) From scripture, we can note that things got progressively worse because of the state of humanity's heart posture. It says *"every intent of the thoughts of his heart was only evil continually. And the Lord was sorry that He made man on earth, and was grieved in His heart. So the Lord said, "I will destroy man who I have created from the face of the earth, both man and beast, creeping thing and birds of the air, for I Am sorry that I made them." But Noah found grace in the eyes of the Lord."*

God is Judgment but He is also Grace. Judgment means to "pronounce an opinion concerning right and wrong." He weighed humanity's actions and judged them as unholy - far from Him and His original intent for us to resemble Him internally; to embody His character. He set the plan to destroy the first line of His creation who, because of sin, embodied unholiness. In the moment that God said that He was sorry he made them (Gen. 6:7), God also repented. I know this is controversial, but we'll discuss that in a later section. However, the scripture says Noah

found grace in the eyes of the Lord (Gen. 6:8). Noah receives this grace, available to him because God is Grace.

Genesis 7
God is a deliverer.

The Judgment resulted in the Flood where the Lord *"destroyed all living things which were on the face of the ground: both man and cattle, creeping thing, and bird of the air. They were destroyed from the earth. Only Noah and those who were with him in the ark remained."* (Gen. 7:22) Then God remembered Noah, stopped the rain, and he was delivered or in simpler terms: rescued from his trial. (Gen. 8:1)

God the Father delivers Noah from the deluge of water and the destruction of all that was behind him, thus He is our Deliverer.

Genesis 8
God is a preparer and a restorer.

Now it was brutal that God drowned the world's population except for Noah and his family. However, God kept Noah on the ark while He restored the earth. When they exited the ark, they would find dry ground and vegetation. In other words, they found sustenance and resources as in Genesis 1 when God created Adam and Eve. Noah and His family were placed in a restored land that was prepared for them as in the original days of creation, except this time they, in obedience to God's command and using the dominion God gave them, brought the animal life that God had preserved. The Word says, *"By the twenty-seventh day of the second month the earth was completely dry. Then God said to Noah, "Come out of the ark, you and your wife and your sons and their wives. Bring out every kind of living creature that is with you—the birds, the animals, and all the creatures that move along the ground—so they can multiply on the earth and be fruitful and increase in number on it."* (Gen. 8:14-17 NIV)

God the Father prepared and restored the land for Noah and his family because God is a Preparer and a Restorer.

Genesis 9:11-15
God is a covenant maker.

In this chapter, God made a covenant with humanity and sent the rainbow as a sign of that covenant. He vowed to never destroy the earth and His people by water again. *"I establish my covenant with you: Never again will all life be destroyed by the waters of a flood; never again will there be a flood to destroy the earth." And God said, "This is the sign of the covenant I am making between me and you and every living creature with you, a covenant for all generations to come: I have set my rainbow in the clouds, and it will be the sign of the covenant between me and the earth."*

God the Father is a covenant making God. Previously, I mentioned that God repented. I know the idea that God repents goes against everything

we know. We say God does not make mistakes. He doesn't. What I can say is that He has a change of heart on matters, especially when we consider the grace that He gives us. But in Genesis 9:11c, God vows to never flood the earth again. He changed His mind and made a vow about not flooding the earth. God repents because He is repentance.

God, Vows, and Covenants

Now, when it comes to vows and covenants, we can stand on Num. 23:19 (NIV): *"God is not human that He should lie, not a human being that He should change His mind. Does He speak and not act? Does He promise and not fulfill?"*

The context of that scripture involved a covenant! Balak the King attempted to have Balaam curse the children of Israel. But God was in covenant with them to bless them and would not change His mind about it. In the case of Noah, God repented out of love for us. With God the Father, we know that His covenant stands.

So what does this have to do with holiness?

Holiness Redefined

When God the Father says, *"Be holy because I, the Lord your God, am holy"* in Lev. 19:2 (NIV), it means holy is who God is; He embodies holiness. If there is holiness to be had, it can only be found in God. The holiness that is required of you, is you being transformed to *be* like God, to *become* or *embody* (not act like or present an image of) the many characteristics of God. Because God is not a puppet master, He doesn't pull strings to make you dance, lift your arm, or walk. Your personality is unique to you and will serve you and others in the kingdom. Unlike the animal kingdom, He created you in His image and likeness - you resemble Him. He created you to have dominion (not to dominate or oppress others), and thus, make decisions as He does. With God, your skills, personality, and decisions are influenced for good, whereas without God, they aren't.

The more you read God's Word and listen for Him, blocking out the noise, the more His character will overtake you. He will buff out some of the hard edges that cut you and those around you...but He will keep the edge that busts the devil's head open. God uses warriors, too! That's what holiness is about.

Holiness is not a stiff-collared one size fits all outfit. It's a daily redirection of the heart through repentance and seeking His way; your crooked paths being made straight. His daily bread will feed you. His voice will become clearer. You will sense when God is redirecting or saying *No, not this*. Or you will sense when an opportunity does not look like the answer you were looking for but God says, *Yes, go forth!* There will be times when you act or are about to act that there is no response one way or the other. One might say His voice quiets as you walk in His ways. The main point is that in holiness, the communication is more intimate.

ೞ

Refills

When you allow God to reign in your heart, your heart will feel a void, at times, that you will only be able to fill with worship. You will feel a pull to sit with Him. Sometimes you will hear the audible invitation. God called Abraham righteous because he believed. And when you thirst for righteousness, for greater belief in God, it will be filled. (Mt. 5:6)

Holiness is about the things of God flowing out of your heart. When your heart is surrendered to God, His will be done. You will be changed by the Holy Spirit that lives in you. Everything else is a copy, a pretense, an attempt at holiness.

Now, let's not throw the scriptural laws away. Laws have a purpose. There are laws in place in the Old Covenant to uphold holiness standards. In Exodus, God coached formerly enslaved people into a new civilization and society. They did not know what holiness was about. They had lived in Egypt for 430 years, and while Hebrew by identity, they likely did not have many worship customs in place prior to leaving Egypt. Remember, God instructs Moses to tell Pharaoh, to let His people go so they can worship Him. (Ex. 5:1, 7:16, 8:1, 8:20, 9:1, 9:13, 10:3) When He appeared to Moses at Mt. Horeb in the burning bush, He advised Moses to remove his shoes on holy ground (Ex. 3:5) because He desires holiness.

This was why he told Moses to keep the children of Israel from touching even the base of Mount Sinai. (Ex. 19:12) His presence was holy and they were not. Those were the Old Covenants, that one had to be holy to come near God. With the coming of Jesus, the New Covenant, things would change.

Who God is: Jesus the Son
Jesus: The New Covenant

Jesus was present in the beginning. (Jn. 1:1-3) God, The Word, became flesh (John 1:14) and fulfilled the law. (Mt. 5:17) Jesus said, *"I am the Way, the Truth, and the Life. No man comes to the Father except through Me."* (Jn. 14:6) If you have accepted Jesus as your Lord and Savior, then you will have access to the Father when following His Way, the Truth of Him (The Word), and His Life. His purpose of coming in the flesh was to die for our sins so we would have eternal life. He became flesh or "became human and made His home among us" (Jn. 1:14, NLT) as an example. This is not an exhaustive list, but a glimpse of how He lived among us.

- **He prayed** (Mt. 14:23, 26:30, 39, 42, 44, Mk. 1:35, 6:46, 14:23, 35, Lk. 5:16, 6:12, 9:28, 11:1, 22:32, 41, 44, Jn.17:1),
- **was baptized** (Mt. 3:13-16, Mk. 1:9-11, Lk. 3:21-23, Jn. 1:29-34),
- **was tempted by Satan and overcame it** (Mt. 4:1-11, Mk. 1:12-13, Lk. 4:1-13),
- **walked the roads amongst the people** (Mt. 4:18+),
- **discipled** (Mt. 4:18-21, Mk. 1:16-20, Lk. 5:1-11+)
- **healed** (Mt. 4:23,24, 8:13,16, 9:22, 12:15, 22, 14:14, 15:28,30, 19:2, 21:14, Mk. 1:34, 3:10, 5:34, 6:56, 10:52, Lk. 4:40, 6:18, Lk.

8:47, 50, 14:4, 17:15, 18:42, 22:51, Jn. 5:9),
- **taught** (Mt. 5:1-7:28, 11:1, Mk. 1:21-22, 2:13, 4:1-2, 6:2, 8:31, 10:1, 11:17, 12:38, Lk. 4:31, 5:3, Jn. 7:14, 8:2)
- **drove out demons** (Mt. 8:32, 17:18, Mk. 1:34, 39, 6:13, 16:9 Lk. 4:41, 8:2, 8:32-33, 9:42),
- **wept** (Jn. 11:35),
- **was betrayed** (Mt. 26:46, 48, 27:3-4, Mk. 14:10, 43-45, Lk. 22:4-6, 47-48, Jn. 13:2, 18:2-5),
- **grieved the weight of His assignment but persevered in the will of the Father** (Mt. 26:38-39, 42, Mk. 14:33-36, Lk. 22:42-44),
- **forgave** (Lk. 23:34),
- **and sacrificed His life** (Mt. 27:46,50, Mk. 15:37, Lk. 23:46, Jn. 19:30).

In all these things, He exhibited love. How generous of God to send His Son, Jesus, as an example of holiness among us. It was not a judge in the land or an elected king, but Jesus, the King of Kings and Lord of Lords (1 Tim 6:15, Rev. 17:14, 19:16) sent to be in our midst. Having seen it, the disciples still got it wrong. Having read it in the Word, we have, too. The difference is that with the Old Covenant, we take off our shoes. But with the New Covenant, the sacrifice is made so we come to God the way we are, shoes on, and Jesus meets us there to redirect us to the Way - His Way.

Jesus: The Way

When we come to Jesus we may ask, like Thomas, *"How can we know the way (His way)?"* (Jn. 14:5) Because even being in His proximity, like His disciples, we get it wrong. But Jesus says, *"I Am the Way, the Truth and the Life. No one comes to the Father except through Me."* (Jn. 14:6, NIV)

If we follow Jesus, who shows the Way - we discover the ways of the Father. When we **do the things Jesus did**, we exhibit the ways of the Father and others experience or witness the ways of the Father through us.

> Jesus said, *"...but He comes so that the world may learn that I love the Father and do exactly what My Father has commanded me. "Come now, let us leave.""* (Jn. 14:31, NIV)

When we **speak how Jesus speaks**, we discover the voice and sound of the Father.

> Jesus said, *"When you have lifted up the Son of Man, then you will know that I am He and that I do nothing on my own but speak just what the Father has taught Me."* (Jn. 8:28, NIV)

> Jesus said, *"I no longer call you servants, because a servant does not know His Father's*

business. Instead, I have called you friends, for everything that I learned from My Father I have made known to you." (Jn. 15:15, NIV)

We get to discover holiness through Jesus.

Jesus the Intentional

Jesus is intentional about us coming to the Father. He is our intercessor. He is our mediator. He is the One who goes out of the way to meet us at the well, wherever it is that we go for temporary fulfillment, in order to offer the Living Water. (Jn. 4:10,14) He showed us how to love as He loved by way of everything He actually did.

Remember how we observed God's character by taking note of what He did in the brief analysis of Genesis? When you are reading the Gospels, you will see God's character through everything Jesus did. Even when we get to Jesus's sacrifice at the cross, we learn that sacrifice is an act of God. God sent His Son to be the sacrifice. Jesus, who despite the heaviness, never lost sight of His assignment and intentions for humanity, agreed in the Garden of Gethsemane to be the sacrifice. (Mt. 26:30,36-46, Mk. 14:26, 32-42, Lk. 22:39-46, John 18:1, Ps. 42:6) What God does is holy. Sacrifice is a part of holiness.

Jesus: The Blueprint of Holiness

Jesus, the Blueprint, left the blueprint of His life to direct each of us because, as we know, His time in the flesh was temporary. He had to go in order to complete His assignment by His crucifixion and resurrection - those things that promised eternal life. (Jn. 3:16)

Do you remember that after Jesus got baptized, the Holy Spirit descended on Him? (Mt. 3:16, Mk. 1:10, Lk. 3:22, Jn. 1:32) Jesus promised that when He left, the Holy Spirit would come. (Jn. 15:26) After His resurrection, He promised again that the Holy Spirit would come upon us and we would have power at that time. (Acts 1:8) The Holy Spirit was then released at Pentecost and they received power! (Acts 2:14) And when we got saved, we received it, too. Why would God send the Holy Spirit? When Jesus in the flesh received the Holy Spirit, He went into the wilderness, and then ministry began. He had received power. With that power, He cast out demons and unclean spirits. If the presence of demons or unclean spirits make us unholy or unclean, then by way of reason, the Holy Spirit - sent by God - makes us holy and clean and gives us power. And as our blueprint, Jesus has modeled for us that we, too, with the Holy Spirit have the power to cast out the unholy. But who is the Holy Spirit?

Who God is: The Holy Spirit
Holy Spirit: Teacher

> *Jesus said, "But the Helper, The Holy Spirit, whom the Father will send in My name, He will teach you all things, and bring to your remembrance all things that I said to you." (Jn. 14:26, NKJV)*

Learning by the Spirit is a gift from God. The revelation that we get when we read scripture, the discernment that comes upon us to identify the holy, the lessons that we learn, the reminders of scripture at the most desperate times or the times that we need guidance is what He promised.

Holy Spirit: Spirit of Truth

> *Jesus said, "...When the Spirit of truth has come, He will guide you into all truth; for He will not speak on His own authority, but whatever He hears He will speak; and He will tell you things to come. He will glorify Me, for He will take of what is Mine and declare it to you. (Jn. 16:13-14, NKJV)*

It's in these moments that the scales fall from your eyes like the Apostle Paul. (Acts 9:18) Where you were once in spiritual darkness, you will now see His Light. His vision for you within the kingdom will begin to materialize. There's more.

Holy Spirit: Power

> *"But you shall receive power when the Holy Spirit has come upon you; and you shall be [c] witnesses to Me in Jerusalem, and in all Judea and Samaria, and to the end of the earth." (Acts 1:8, NKJV)*

You will be empowered to tell of who Christ is and what He's done: that He went to the cross for us and was resurrected from the dead just as we have been raised in Him. You will freely tell how He is available to those who desire to be saved, to be healed and made whole. When the Spirit comes upon you, you will be filled with His Spirit and be able to speak in other tongues as the Holy Spirit gives you utterance. (Acts 2:4) He will unify language contrary to the confusion of languages at the Tower of Babel (Genesis 11). In other words, this is not just about speaking in tongues, but those filled with and unified by the Spirit will understand one another.

Holy Spirit: Prophecy

> *"And it shall come to pass in the last days, says God, That I will pour out My Spirit on all flesh; Your sons and your daughters shall prophesy, Your young men shall see visions, Your old men shall dream dreams..."*
> (Joel 2:28, Acts 2:17)

As prophesied by the prophet Joel, with the Holy Spirit, sons and daughters will hear the Word that God speaks, see what God desires to show us while awake and in slumber, and be able to convey it to the intended receiver(s). It is God's intention to get His Word and plans to His children for the sake of the kingdom. His Spirit within us, is the means.

ଔ

Holy Spirit: A Mind Governed by The Spirit of God

Speaking God's message is not the sum total of God's desire for the Spirit. Romans 8:1-8 (NIV) delves deeper into why the Holy Spirit was sent.

> *8 Therefore, there is now no condemnation for those who are in Christ Jesus, 2 because through Christ Jesus the law of the Spirit who gives life has set you[a] free from the law of sin and death. 3 For what the law was powerless to do because it was weakened by the flesh,[b] God did by sending his own Son in the likeness of sinful flesh to be a sin offering.[c] And so he condemned sin in the flesh, 4 in order that the righteous requirement of the law might be fully met in us, who do not live according to the flesh but according to the Spirit. 5 Those who live according to the flesh have their minds set on what the flesh desires; but those who live in accordance with the Spirit have their minds set on what the Spirit desires. 6 The mind governed by the flesh is death, but the mind governed by the Spirit is life and peace. 7 The mind governed by the flesh is hostile to God; it does not submit to God's law, nor can it do so. 8 Those who are in the realm of the flesh cannot please God.*

The Holy Spirit draws us to God's desires; that being life and peace. Paul explains that once you come to Jesus you are not condemned to death as the law had once decreed. Think about the children of Israel who did not keep the Lord's commandments or the kings who did not do right in the eyes of the Lord. They had the law, and yet, could not always follow through. They were consistently being given into the hands of their enemies. They wanted to be delivered from their enemies and hardship but they were resistant to doing things God's way. The flesh was the captain of the team and led all the plays which led them to dire consequences that included captivity, exile, and death. When we meet Daniel, Nebuchadnezzar, King of Babylon has overcome Zedekiah, King of Judah (Jer. 52:10-11) and has overtaken and destroyed Jerusalem (Jer. 52:12-23), and has taken captives. (Jer. 52:24-30)

Daniel and friends served in the king's palace because their people displeased God and had been taken captive. (Dan. 1:1-6) Jehoiakim was a prisoner in exile for 37 years. (Jer. 52:31) There were priests who *"strove against Moses and against Aaron in the company of Korah, when they strove against the Lord"* and were swallowed up into the earth. They had the law. And perished. (Num. 26:10) We would be no different, except we have the sacrifice of Christ. God is a Redeemer, He forgives, and has given the gift of repentance.

We've had the law all along, but it's the Spirit that does the changing. That's why He sent the Holy Spirit and holiness can prevail.

☙

The Holy Spirit and Your Walk

In Galatians 5:16-18 (NKJV), the apostle Paul explained how you should partner with the Spirit of God, the Holy Spirit, and why. He wrote,

> *"I say then, "Walk in the Spirit and you shall not fulfill the lust of the flesh. For the flesh lusts against the Spirit, and the Spirit against the flesh; and these are contrary to one another, so that you do not do the things that you wish. But if you are led by the Spirit, you are not under the law."*

Paul has already said a similar thing about the battle between the flesh and Spirit in Romans 8:1-8, but in this scripture, let's focus on the word, "walk." The Greek word for walk is *peripateo*. It means to make one's way. The Hebrew word for one's walk is *halak* which translates to "to live", "to regulate one's life," or "to conduct one's self." It is also a figure of speech for the manner in which one lives. So Paul's instruction is for us to regulate one's life by allowing the Holy Spirit to lead, and that way your flesh will not lead you astray. In a nutshell, partnering with the Holy Spirit is always going to lead you to holiness.

When God told Moses to take off His shoes in Ex. 3:5, God established that He is holy; set apart from humankind's walk or the manner in which humanity lives. God, however, is not apart from them in a way that means He is far away or uninvolved. Moses could not wear the shoes that walked in the way of men. In God's presence, holiness was required.

However, when Jesus left, God sent the Holy Spirit to all who believed so we, too, would separate from the manner in which unbelievers live (i.e. customs, idol worship, the profane), but remain witnesses to the goodness of Christ - loving as He did.

Holiness or being set apart is not being prideful where you think you are better than others. It is not getting someone saved to get a notch on your own holiness belt. Rather, holiness is about your heart's desire to see them saved. It's you seeing how Abraham bargained with God for the souls of sinners, interceding the same way (Gen. 18:20-32), and asking God how to minister to them. It's knowing He saved you from the life you were living and instead of looking down on others, desiring to offer someone else the opportunity to know Christ, the same source of your new peace. The Holy Spirit empowers and partners with you to do this. (Acts 1:8) This is holiness in action.

> Romans 12:1 (NIV) says, *"Therefore, I urge you, brothers and sisters, in view of God's mercy, to offer your bodies as a living sacrifice, holy and pleasing to God—this is your true and proper worship."*

When your body has become a living sacrifice, the flesh has been placed on the altar. It is then that we become holy and pleasing to God. This is when the Spirit takes precedence over the flesh; what we desire or prefer. Some say *Hallelujah* is the highest praise, but becoming a living sacrifice far surpasses that. This worship surpasses even the most beautifully choreographed praise dance and angelic choir. This worship is peak holiness.

One more thing....

1 John 4:16-21 (NIV) says,

> *"And so we know and rely on the love God has for us. God is Love. Whoever lives in love, lives in God, and God in them. This is how love is made complete among us so that we will have confidence on the day of judgment: In this world we are like Jesus. There is no fear in love. But perfect love drives out fear. Because fear has to do with punishment. The one who fears is not made perfect in love. We love because He first loved us. Whoever claims to love God yet hates a brother or sister is a liar. For whoever does not love their brother or sister, whom they have seen, cannot love God, whom they have not seen. And He has given us this command: Anyone who loves God must also love their brother and sister."*

Period.

God's Love is at the center of holiness. Holiness begets Love. You see how that works? Holiness requires God's will, that we remain in Him. To remain in Him is to remain in His Word, pray without ceasing (stay in communication with Him) per 1 Thess. 5:17, love God with all your heart, and love your neighbors. (Mt. 22:37-39) We must remain in Him because the Word says, "Apart from Me you can do nothing." (Jn. 15:5) That includes love.

You can have the tallest, pearliest, most bedazzled church hat or the finest in luxury leather loafers. But if your walk, *peripateo*, or manner of living does not include love then your walk lacks holiness.

We've gotten a grasp on understanding God's character and how it relates to holiness. Now let's get into how God sees us in order to have a more acute understanding of holiness.

Who You Are to God

Old Covenant

HUMANITY WAS CREATED HOLY by the Holy God. God called creation good, but when creation included Adam and Eve, He called creation very good (Gen. 1:31). They had no accomplishments, nor had they impressed Him in any way. They were very good for the simple fact that they were created beings made in His image and likeness. Very good is the equivalent to high value.

The psalmist notes that human creation is fearfully and wonderfully made. (Psalm 139:14) The Hebrew word for fearful is *yare* (pronounced yaw-ray) which is translated into reverence. Fearful does not mean full of fear, but inspired by awe and reverence. The Hebrew word for wonderful is *palah* which is translated as: to distinguish/set apart or marvelous. Wonderful means as a created being you are full of wonder. You are made magnificently.

Adam and Eve were created, just as you and I were, in

the image and likeness of God. Because of sin, we were separated from Him. That's our story. Yet, God is so far beyond measure and constraints that it is entirely possible for each of us to be made in His image and still be unique. Still, we resemble God most when we follow His way!

Humankind was created holy. God gave Adam and Eve, as He gave you and me, dominion. Having dominion meant you would always be able to make decisions as to where your allegiance lies. Adam and Eve chose an allegiance to themselves. And that's when they saw their own nakedness. Nudity was not shameful. Humanity was birthed in its natural state as the animals were. The nakedness they saw was their own shame and embarassment. It was similar to having a clothing malfunction in public, but the audience was God. Because of their decision, we were conceived in sin (Ps. 51:5), thus we are sinners by nature. From the day we were born, we were exposed to the world and its wicked ways. Still, God did not forsake us.

In the Old Covenant, He created you and called you very good. (Gen. 1:31) He said you were fearfully and wonderfully made. (Ps. 139:14) He said you were chosen to be his treasured possession. (Deut. 14:2) The Old Covenant was revelation of our sinful nature and an attempt to build the character of the children of Israel by establishing order and discipline for their new lives in Him. If I may say so without incurring the arrows, the old covenant also highlights the limitations the law has in transforming a people. (See Israel.)

08

New Covenant

The New Covenant, however, explores a greater *partnership* with God that was previously designated for a select group of leaders, but expanded to include all who believe in Jesus Christ. In John 6:48-50 (NIV), Jesus says,

> *"I am the bread of life. Your ancestors ate the manna in the wilderness, yet they died. But here is the bread that comes down from heaven, which anyone may eat and not die."*

In the wilderness, there was a provision given to the children of Israel to manage for a season. There is, however, an eternal provision in this New Covenant named Christ; a daily bread for daily sustenance until He returns. It's an authority that is not found in the Old Testament. It is filled with the possibility of maturation and empowerment as co-laborers with Christ (2 Cor. 6:1) establishing God's kingdom...in holiness. When Jesus went to the cross, the veil of the temple was torn from top to bottom (Mt. 27:51, Mk. 15:38, Lk. 23:45) and taken away.(2 Cor. 3:16) There was no longer a separation from God as with the Old Covenant.

With the tearing from the top to the bottom - from the heavens to the earth, we know the tearing was an act of God. We were given access to the Holy of Holies or the Most Holy Place. (Heb. 9:3, AMP, NIV respectively)

At the cross, with the sacrifice of the Lamb who takes

away the sin of the world (John 1:29), holiness became attainable for all who believe.

Who You Are in Christ

WHEN YOU ACCEPT CHRIST, NOT JUST as Savior, but Lord of your life, your identity changes. The world will try to give you funky names: Bible Thumper, Holy Roller, Jesus Freak. They will call you these things because the resemblance to and radiance of God is too much to take in and the need to belittle or humble you has risen up. Conversely, people before you may have been nasty or unkind; bearing no reflection of God.

What they call you has nothing to do with who Jesus says you are. Jesus gives each of us a new identity. If you don't know who God says you are, your identity can be shaped by those who have no idea who you've been created to be. This is how one can be steered away from holiness toward churchiness that is powerless to change. So who does He say you are?

You are a Disciple

When you decide to follow Christ and learn His ways, you become a disciple. The Greek word for disciple is *math-*

etes. It means a learner or a pupil.

Jesus walked along the road and called regular people, like you and me, into His service. The first of these were fishermen who dropped their nets to follow Him. He walked (both literally and figuratively) with the disciples, lived among them, taught them, encouraged them, and admonished them. He invited them into a premier mentorship program like no other. I should mention, by the way, that some of these disciples were women. They were not part of the twelve, but they were present. Some were benefactors, some were at the cross, at the tomb, saw Him resurrected, and were in the upper room at Pentecost. All were learners and pupils. As disciples today, He mentors us by His word and by divinely appointed relationships. Holiness comes out of proper discipleship.

You are His Friend

"No longer do I call you servants, for a servant does not know what his master is doing; but I have called you friends, for all things that I heard from My Father I have made known to you." (Jn. 15:15, NKJV)

When we give our lives to Christ and follow Him wholeheartedly as disciples - learners and pupils - our status with Him changes over time. God begins to reveal Himself more definitively. When we don't follow wholeheartedly, it doesn't. We remain servants. This is why we can serve at church, but never see a move of God or hear from Him - we have no idea what the Master is doing. If we simply serve at church and get recognition and accolades from humans, that is our reward. But when we serve at church *and* diligently seek the Bread of Life, our spirit, eyes, ears, and hearts, are primed for friendship. We know what the Master is doing. What is instructed by the Father, Christ tells us in His Word. It jumps off the page and resonates deeply. What is perceived is revealed to us via the Holy Spirit either audibly or by an unexplainable knowing - the way friends sometimes know what the other is thinking. With this friendship, we begin to look alike, us taking on the likeness of Christ in His ways. Holiness pours out in our speech and actions, pushing back the sinful nature which attempts to rise up at any given time. The sinful nature loses its power the more we seek and abide in Christ, in His divine nature. In some ways we become unfamiliar to those who knew us when. As friends of Christ Divine, holiness abounds.

You are A New Creation

If you are in Christ, the New Covenant, He calls you a new creation. (2 Cor. 5:17) When Jesus meets Nicodemus the Pharisee, a ruler of the Jews in John 3:1-2, Jesus tells him that in order to see the kingdom of heaven he must be born again. (Jn. 3:3) This great teacher of high status is confused because as a grown man, how can he return to the womb? But Jesus explains that we must be born again by water and by Spirit. Born again is another term for new creation. It's like being a new baby, but a new baby born of Christ. Now, over the years we have come to the understanding that being born by water is being baptized as Jesus was. But there's more. In the following chapter, in John 4:13-15 (NIV), Jesus invites the woman at the well to drink of the Living Water, that she would never thirst again, and she says yes.

"13 Jesus answered, "Everyone who drinks this water will be thirsty again, 14 but whoever drinks the water I give them will never thirst. Indeed, the water I give them will become in them a spring of water welling up to eternal life." 15 The woman said to him, "Sir, give me this water so that I won't get thirsty and have to keep coming here to draw water."

It is in the kingdom of heaven that we experience "eternal life;" the same kingdom of heaven that Jesus describes to Nicodemus in John 3:3. We cannot get to the kingdom of heaven as the old creations we once were. But with this Living Water, eternal life in the kingdom of heaven is ours. So Jesus offers it and she says, *Yes. Give it here, Sir.* When you accept the Living Water, you are a new creation, born in Christ, who will never thirst. Holiness abounds here.

You are a Temple of the Living God

Scripture asks *"And what agreement has the temple of God with idols? For you[a] are the temple of the living God. As God has said: I will dwell in them and walk among them. I will be their God and they will be My people."* (2 Co. 6:16, NKJV) In the Old Testament, the Spirit of God was housed in the Ark of the Covenant. A man named Uzzah (2 Sam. 6:6-7) was killed because he touched the outside, the casing, the container which carried the presence of the Lord, the Most High God. And yet, we are considered a temple of the Living God. God places His Spirit on the inside of us. The Greek word for temple (*naos*) used in this scripture refers to a sanctuary, but more specifically the inner part of it.[21] The Holy Spirit is held within us, in the inner part. We are a resting place. Imagine the value God places on us in allowing us to house His Spirit. Just like in the house of worship, God is worshiped based on our actions. Or He can be ignored based on our actions. Holiness abounds in worship of God who is within us.

You are a Living Stone, a Spiritual House, a Holy Priesthood (1 Peter 2:5)

Jesus is the Cornerstone. When building the house, or in this case, the kingdom of heaven, every stone has to be the right fit. The Cornerstone was made from "the stone the builders rejected." (Mk. 12:10, NIV) This is the foundation on which we build our faith. In His resurrection, Jesus made it possible for us to be the living stones, malleable by Him, yet steadfast and filled with His Holy Spirit that would build up the church. Paul S. Minear asserts that "Each stone is now viewed as a priest and each priest as a stone."[22] In being those stones, we, again, become a house for the Spirit to live in. "This house is spiritual because indwelt by the Holy Spirit. Its char-

---

21   Vine's Expository Dictionary of New Testament Words.
22   Paul S. Minear, The House of Living Stones: A Study of 1 Peter 2:4-12, The Ecumenical Review, 242.

acter is determined by the Spirit;"[3] And when the Holy Spirit has rest in us, we, a priesthood called into His service, become holy. "This priesthood is holy because of the work within it of the Holy Spirit...The holiness of this priesthood resides not in institutions but in persons and in their activity as stones."[4] Holiness abounds in the church built of the living stones.

You are Chosen, Royal, Holy, and Special

> *"But you are a chosen generation, a royal priesthood, a holy nation, His own special people, that you may proclaim the praises of Him who called you out of the darkness into His marvelous light;"* (1 Pt. 2:9, NKJV)

God called Israel chosen, but they missed the mark. Their disobedience put them in exile, away from Him. But Jesus has chosen us to be a priesthood, royal in our service to the King of Kings and invited back into His court. As His people, inhabited by the Holy Spirit, we are a holy nation. Our citizenship is in the kingdom of heaven where we no longer walk in darkness - neither in sin nor lack of knowledge - but in the Light of His goodness and mercy that follows us all the days of our lives. (Ps. 23:6) Holiness abounds in His marvelous Light.

ଓଃ

---

[3] Minear, 242.
[4] Ibid.

You are the Branches

God calls us the branches because this is who we are in Him. He is the Vine, we are the branches, (Jn. 15:5, NIV) while the Father is the vinedresser who cuts off the branches (us) that bear no fruit and prunes the branches of those who do. (Jn. 15:1-2, NIV) As the branch connected to the Vine, the nutrients of His Spirit course through us; the branches bearing fruit to successfully navigate the Life in Him. Fruit sprouts within us. The fruit on the branches are sweet fruit to be digested and simultaneously expressed by us. But when we separate from the Vine, the Father gets to work. He cuts the dead leaves off the branches until the proper fruit sprouts and we regain the connection. Love, joy, peace, patience, kindness, goodness, faithfulness, gentleness, and self-control (Gal. 5:22-23) become the fruit that is evidence that holiness abounds.

When you know who God says you are and learn who you are in Christ, your identity is better established; a foundation is laid. When you choose to make Jesus your Lord and Savior, old things of the world will fall away; some things you will lose the taste for and some things require the diligence of choosing daily. The Word says, *"the devil left Him until an opportune time"* (Lk. 4:13) meaning Satan is always waiting for an opportunity so you must make the decision to choose God daily.

Whether or not you choose Him can be influenced by how you view yourself, how much weight you place on who

God says you are, and how much He is a part of you. The very important part is that it is God who tells you who you are, not the world, and not man. The bread of life (Jn. 6:48) is not found in doctrines of holy garments and false modesty. His bread is His love, His wisdom, and His voice overriding the loudness of sin and the call of the flesh.

The road to holiness always comes back to these questions: *Will you eat the food of this world and die or will you eat the daily bread, drink of the Living Water, and live holy?*

This was God's intention from the start of creation: holiness.

When we understand who God truly is, His identity as Father, Son, and Holy Spirit, His character, who we are to Him, who He says we are, we are in a new place of understanding. It is here that we prosper. It is here that the pure heart emerges and flourishes.

The Pure Heart

PROVERBS 6:12-19 (NIV) SAYS,

> *A troublemaker and a villain, who goes about with a corrupt mouth, 13 who winks maliciously with his eye, signals with his feet and motions with his fingers, 14 who plots evil with deceit in his heart— he always stirs up conflict. 15 Therefore disaster will overtake him in an instant; he will suddenly be destroyed—without remedy. 16 There are six things the Lord hates, seven that are detestable to him: 17 haughty eyes, a lying tongue, hands that shed innocent blood, 18 a heart that devises wicked schemes, feet that are quick to rush into evil, 19 a false witness who pours out lies, and a person who stirs up conflict in the community.*

The pure heart is the opposite. The pure heart is goals.

The pure heart is not perfect, but it desires to be perfected in Christ - the author and perfecter of our faith. (Heb. 12:2, NET) The pure heart is not always visible to the naked eye. The pure heart is not a strict rule follower and rule enforcer that lives a black and white life filled with restrictions. Rather, it is surrendered to the will of God and understands the gray areas of mercy and kindness to the unmerciful and unkind. The pure heart seeks to fill up on the Word. It desires the Spirit of Truth to be the captain of its ship. When the Spirit of Truth is allowed to lead, the fruit of the Spirit becomes evident not just to themselves but to others. The pure heart understands that obedience is better than sacrifice. (1 Sam. 16:22) And in the case of disobedience or error, it is repentant. It seeks to make things right with God.

Paul says:

> *"Finally, brethren, whatsoever things are true, whatsoever things are honest, whatsoever things are just, whatsoever things are pure, whatsoever things are lovely, whatsoever things are of good report; if there be any virtue, and if there be any praise, think on these things."* (Phil. 4:8, NKJV)

These things fill and fuel the pure heart. The virtue that the scripture speaks of is the Greek word *arete* which means moral goodness or moral excellence. When these true, honest, just, pure, lovely things are what we think about, ponder, or study, these are the things that fill the heart. Whenever we fill the heart with all this goodness according to biblical standards, that is what first changes us, then is poured out on our families, our communities, our cities, states, and more. That is when we are most like Christ. That is when His love is shared.

What else feeds the heart?

The Bread of Life

Jesus says, *I am the Bread of Life*. (Jn. 6:48) He also teaches us to pray *"Give us this day our Daily Bread."* (Mt. 6:11) Jesus can download just about anything He pleases during our daily prayers. But our main source of Bread is the Word, the Old and New Covenant, that fills us up and give us sustenance. When we are filled with the Word, we hide it in our hearts so that we do not sin against God. (Ps. 119:10) We don't have to know the scriptures verbatim. The Holy Spirit will call it to remembrance. (Jn. 14:26)

The Holy Spirit

> *"In his sermon Scriptural Christianity, Wesley identifies the extraordinary gifts as the "gift of healing, of working other miracles, of prophecy, of discerning spirits, the speaking with divers kinds of tongues, and the interpretation of tongues." Wesley adds that not everyone had*

these gifts, "perhaps one in a thousand." However, the gift of the Holy Spirit was "for a more excellent purpose": the cultivation of the "ordinary fruits," which are "essential to all Christians in all ages." [23]

Many Black Church congregations place high value on the extraordinary gifts. While it's wonderful to have the extraordinary fruit, John Wesley, the Father of the Methodist Church contends that to have the ordinary fruit is better as it is essential to all. It's the ordinary fruits, the characteristics of God that are seen in daily interactions. Throughout the Word, God exhibited the fruit of the Spirit, the first of which is love, followed by joy, peace, patience, kindness, goodness, faithfulness, gentleness, and self-control - because He is those things. The fruit is a sign of holiness because Jesus embodied and exhibited it. This was His way. These things, the fruit of the Spirit according to Galatians 5:22-23 are clear manifestations of God's love developing within us and pouring out of us. It is the evidence of walking by the Spirit of God.

The fruit is only evident when the Holy Spirit is given reign in one's heart. When the Holy Spirit is given reign and has been allowed to flow, pride, lust, envy, gluttony, rage are neutralized. Only then can holiness preside. Wesley was asked, *"What is the best proof of being led by the Spirit?" He responded, "A thorough change and renovation of mind and*

---

23 https://firebrandmag.com/articles/wesley-the-almost-charismatic

heart, and the leading a new and holy life."[24]

While the extraordinary gifts do not necessarily indicate the leading of a holy life, the fruit of the Spirit is more concrete in identifying holiness. It allows us to live well with our sisters and brothers in Christ. We, as the Black Church, can cultivate and maintain healthy relationships and work together to stomp out the plans of the enemy when holiness abounds. This is the purpose of the remix: so holiness may flourish.

Generational curses are broken in this place. Abusive cycles are broken in this place. Bondage is broken in this place. Sin is no longer the slaveholder of the soul in this place. When these things are broken, we are transformed; restored to the intended model. We embody and emanate the Spirit of God which is evidenced by our fruit.

This is the holiness that is still right. This is the holiness that God desires of His church - the Black Church and otherwise. It's where He'd like us to return. This holiness starts in our hearts; transforming us. We receive the mind of Christ. We see ourselves and others through His lens. This holiness first pervades the church, then seeps out into the world. The world then receives the Good News of Christ in how we live, not just the things we pronounce. Putting on the show of holiness dies. The world sees God through the love we share.

And God gets the glory.

---

24   https://firebrandmag.com/articles/wesley-the-almost-charismatic

Final Words

THE WORLD DOESN'T SEE OUR Jesus t-shirts or churchy clothes or robes or church lingo or shouting as holy or godly. They see us as "one of them" meaning one of those church people, when in fact we may be as worldly internally as they are.

It's not, never has been, nor will it ever be enough to be seen as one of them. In church spaces we learn how to navigate world spaces. But if we're playing at holiness, we will play at it outside the church, as well. We will navigate the church and world by churchy standards being seen as, but not *being or embodying* holiness.

Peter, like each of us, was seen as one of them, but denied Christ. His denial was in word, ours in word, action, or both. Like him, we must repent. (Mt. 26:75) And instead of being seen as, we must actually *be* one of them who, empowered by the Holy Spirit, has been changed. We must *be* one of them who goes out preaching Good News to the poor (in spirit, truth, health, and finance), witnessing like the Woman at the Well who said, *"Come and see a Man who knew every-*

thing I'd ever done!"

Sharing The Good News of Jesus Christ, of what He's done - that He saved each of us both now and for eternity - brings hope to the hopeless. When we tell of how He healed us mentally, spiritually, and emotionally from centuries of experiences meant to kill us; restored spiritual sight to world-blinded eyes and hearing to world-deafened ears; brought us out of destitution - these and those like it are the testimonies that, with the blood of the Lamb, help each of us and others overcome! This is holiness!

In holiness, you will find the courage to break that chain of trying to appear as anything other than yourself - a Black person made in the image and likeness of God. Are we sinless? No. But we have the ability to repent.

This. Is. Holiness.

In holiness, we will no longer be a powerless church, but will speak the word of the Lord and see miracles happen. Our prayers will reach heaven and the power of God will be seen in the lives of those who did not previously believe. And the glory will be His. When we don't "do" holiness, but embody holiness, it is then that people see God. They see the wisdom and truth along with supernatural power. The dreams we dream and the words we hear by the Spirit will be the warning or counsel needed for His purposes, not our own.

We will know what to say, when to speak against systems of oppression and when to stand down. We will know how to resist the devil so he will flee, and when to go to war against the thief who comes to steal, kill, and destroy; not just for ourselves, but for the good of our neighbors because holiness is collective. It's not only about us.

With holiness, even with holiness, and in spite of holiness, sin will rise up because you are still human and the devil returns at an opportune time. (Lk. 4:13) That's his job. You may feel the urge to say or do something you shouldn't and in that moment, the Holy Spirit who has been resting in the house will rise up and say, *"Don't."*

You'll hear it and feel it. You may cover your mouth to gain a few moments. That may be the extent of His communication on the matter. Or very softly, you'll hear His whisper of a new command. At that moment, you have a choice.

It's not the Bible or the Proverbs 31 mug on your desk, but Your response to God's voice that determines holiness - regardless of how anyone else perceives you. At that moment, The Holy Spirit has offered you victory over the flesh. This is holiness. And if you fail, and repent, it's still holiness.

This remix was never intended to change the song, but to introduce you to a new rhythm in Christ. Moving to His beat by the leading of the Holy Spirit. Is it easy? No. Is it necessary in order to live in the way God desires? Absolutely.

Works Cited

Barna Group. "Millions of Unchurched Adults Are Christians Hurt by Churches but Can Be Healed of the Pain." Barna Group, 5 Dec. 2023, www.barna.com/research/millions-of-unchurched-adults-are-christians-hurt-by-churches-but-can-be-healed-of-the-pain/.

Bellini, Peter J. "Wesley, the Almost Charismatic." Firebrand Magazine, Firebrand Magazine, 6 Dec. 2022, firebrandmag.com/articles/wesley-the-almost-charismatic.

Cone, James H. The Cross and the Lynching Tree. United States, Orbis Books, 2011.

Ealey, Shani. "Literacy by Any Means Necessary: The History of Anti-Literacy Laws in the U.S." Oakland Literacy Coalition, 29 Jan. 2024, oaklandliteracycoalition.org/literacy-by-any-means-necessary-the-history-of-anti-literacy-laws-in-the-u-s/#.

Lynne, Sandra. "Black Church Culture and Community Action." Social Forces (2005): n. pag. Print. pp. 967-94.

David Guzik Commentary/Study Guide for Matthew 23.

Minear, Paul S. "The House of Living Stones." The Ecumenical Review, vol. 34, no. 3, July 1982, pp. 238–248, https://doi.org/10.1111/j.1758-6623.1982.tb03364.x.

Montgomery, Harry Earl. Vital American Problems: An Attempt to Solve the Trust, Labor, and Negro Problems. United Kingdom, Putnam, 1908.

PBS. Slavery and the Making of America . the Slave Experience: Religion | PBS, www.thirteen.org/wnet/slavery/experience/religion/history2.html.

Walker, Clarence E. "The A.M.E. Church and Reconstruction." Negro History Bulletin, vol. 48, no. 1, 1985, pp. 10–12. JSTOR, http://www.jstor.org/stable/44176613. Accessed 24 July 2024.

Vine's Expository Dictionary of New Testament Words.

www.ingramcontent.com/pod-product-compliance
Lightning Source LLC
Chambersburg PA
CBHW071126090426
42736CB00012B/2029